STRAIGHT TO GAY

COMING OUT SAVED MY LIFE
- CREATING JOY AND HEALTH

AUDREY KOUYOUMDJIAN

10-10-10
Publishing

Straight To Gay
Coming Out Saved My Life, Creating Joy and Health
straighttogaybook.com
Copyright © 2017 Audrey Kouyoumdjian

ISBN: 978-1-77277-196-1

Publisher
10-10-10 Publishing
Markham, ON
Canada

Printed in Canada and the United States of America

TABLE OF CONTENTS

Testimonials

I have always admired my friend Audrey Kouyoumdjian's positive spirit, desire to be involved, and need to make a difference. Audrey has taken the difficulties of her coming out story and presented them with kind sincerity and openness. She will convince you that telling the truth, and living life lovingly, is healing, saves lives, and creates joy and health.

Kathleen Wynne, Premier of Ontario

Straight to Gay is a page-turner, demonstrating how Audrey Kouyoumdjian turned her life challenges into victories. By sharing her highly personal coming out experience, Audrey Kouyoumdjian has made an important contribution to the welfare of all those with any kind of cross to bear. Her story is wonderfully written, and her life is a testament to the creation of joy and health.

Reverend Brent Hawkes, Senior Pastor of The Metropolitan Community Church of Toronto, Order of Canada

This inspiring story leads us on an emotional journey towards living a truthful and joyful life. A real life, coming out biography, the author details her anguish and struggles as she tries to understand her feelings. Her revelations demonstrate the strength, courage, and commitment of one woman as she confronts decades of keeping a deeply held secret, while leading a double life. The author's eventual decision to face her darkest fears forces her to deal with the ramifications in her life (from family and friends, to the community, and her own livelihood) and produces a tsunami of stunning and unexpected responses. In the end, her journey leads us to one conclusion: "we all want to love and be loved." Hard to put down, no matter what your lifestyle, the author shares principles that can help each of us achieve our best genuine selves.

Karen Rucas B.Sc.O.T. Reg (Ont), Occupational Therapist and Certified Life Care Planner

Kouyoumdjian invites the reader—with uncommon grace, warmth, and honesty—to share in her amazing life. Reading this book is like chatting with your seatmate on a long flight or train trip. You always thought you knew all about people but then realize how much more there is to discover... and how fascinating life can be. Pick up the book, and join Kouyoumdjian in her journey and, thereby, perhaps surprisingly, brighten and enlighten your own.

Thomas Klassen, Professor, York University, Toronto

Dedication

I dedicate this book to my daughters, Nicole, Tania, and Gabi, for it is their devoted love and constant laughter that sustains my joy and health.

This book is also dedicated to my partner, Carol, and her children, Michael, Daniel, and Barbara, who have always shown me loving kindness.

Foreword

I first met Audrey Kouyoumdjian when she came to my seminar, Create Your Own Economy. When I first heard the beginning of Audrey's story, I was interested to hear more. I felt honoured to be the first one to help coach her as she experienced the pleasure of writing her book *Straight to Gay, Coming Out Saved My Life, Creating Joy and Health* and then noticed how her writing journey enhanced her life.

Audrey's story is compelling because she herself lived through periods of anguish and sickness while at the same time creating joy and health. Her book points to her secretive double life when dealing with fears and awkward situations, as well as her wanted and unwanted feelings of love and hidden emotions. Family, friends and children further add to the layered complexity of her story. While secretly in love with a woman when married to her husband, Kouyoumdjian was forced to dance around the truth causing her stress, pain, and illness, until her near death surgery created an epiphany that would save her life. She had the steadfast gift of remaining positive and seeing the good whenever she was confronted with fears, illnesses and barriers.

By sharing her own positive reactions during her frequent moves, health issues and the discovery of her sexuality, Audrey shows you that you can create your own joy and health in the midst of any difficulty. It is all here: honest expression, serious purpose, fearlessness and the wanting of love. Audrey's passion to ease the way for you is evident on every page. Her words will resonate with you if you've ever felt alone, awkward, or needing to hide something.

If any part of this book is relevant to you, it will put a positive spin on your most difficult challenges. You will be unable to put the book down. The inspiration and understanding of how Audrey decided to come out will change your life.

Whether you are a member of the LGBTQ community or you have a family member or loved one who is, reading this book will show you how to avoid a difficult life that could cause illness, hurt and sadness. Audrey shows you how 'coming out' can save your life, and create joy and health.

Raymond Aaron
New York Times Bestselling Author

Acknowledgements

Thank you to the **readers** who will live to create their own joy and health.

Thank you to my parents, **Hachy and Dorothy Horasan,** for my *happy genes* that provided me with rose coloured glasses to see the good side of everything.

Thank you to my sister, **Wendy Walters,** who genuinely smiled, and inspired me to do the same, as she forged through her own challenges, until she sadly died in 2016, at the age of 68.

A special thanks to my sister **Chris Papazian,** who has always been the caring one, with both feet solidly on the ground. I'm forever comforted knowing that she will always love me and have my back.

There are no words to express my gratitude for my daughters, **Nicole, Tania, and Gabrielle Kouyoumdjian,** who are the reason I feel joy and love in my life. Their never ending love always gave me a reason to smile, and their quiet support gave me strength as I navigated through the tougher times.

Thank you to **Raffi Kouyoumdjian,** who provided many years of happiness, and for being a fantastic dad to our 3 amazing daughters, even when our family was on shaky ground. Although we are now divorced, I consider Him an important part of my family.

A loving thank you to Carol's mother, **Mynne Pasternak**, and her children, **Michael, Daniel, and Barbara Fagan,** and Carol's brothers, **Stanley and Harvey Pasternak,** and their families, who have always loved and supported Carol, and have shown warmth and kindness to include me in their lives, allowing the blending of our families into a modern family.

Thank you to **Brent Hawkes** and The Metropolitan Community Church, who came into my life at a time when I needed inspirational spiritual teaching, volunteering advocating, and giving back contributions, and friendships, in the LGBTQ community.

Thank you so much to my **long-time friends,** who I so deeply cherish, even more today. We will be connected for a lifetime; I couldn't be more certain of that.

Thank you, **friends of my past.** We were great while we lasted. You were in my life for a reason. I've gone from bitter to better.

Thank you to the many **women in our support group** who provided raw, memorable coming out stories that taught me so much as I was understanding how to come out myself—a win–win, 12-year journey.

A wholehearted thank you to my many **new friends,** whom I hold dearly, LGBTQ and straight, you know who you are.

Thank you to my **patients,** whose questions and goals demanded that I provide the best physiotherapy treatment, while giving me a sense of purpose. I always felt challenged to do my very best to maximize their health.

Acknowledgements

Thank you to 2 wonderful friends for your endorsements: **Premier Kathleen Wynne**, and **Rev. Brent Hawkes**, who have both provided me with inspiration while I was writing, and determination to advocate.

Thank you to my friends, **Thomas Klassen** and **Karen Rucas**, for adding invaluable comments, encouragement, and beautiful testimonials within my chapters.

Thank you to **Dean Tomlinson Photography** who took the candid cover photo while I was marching in the parade.

Thank you to **Justine Apple Photography** for my head shot.

Many, many thanks to **Raymond Aaron**, who is an incredible teacher, coach, and inspirational speaker. Also, to his team in the **Raymond Aaron Group,** for providing me the opportunity to tell my story, to improve lives.
Book Architect – **Cara Witvoet**
Editor – **Lisa Browning**

An extraordinary huge thank you to my partner, **Carol Pasternak,** who led me and helped glide me through my transition from straight to gay. We held one another's hand, and pulled each other along through our loving journey, creating joy each step of the way. I wouldn't have been able to write this book without her loving encouragement and support, or our brainstorming, and knowing that it was the right thing for me to do.

This list would not be complete without a special acknowledgement of **Her**, who sat beside me on the rollercoaster of life and love for so many years. I am forever grateful to **Her**, beyond words.

Chapter 1

Making Sense of it All

What's in a Journey?

Once upon a time is the beginning of a fairy-tale. This is, by far, not a fairy-tale, because it's not a fantasy but very real. It's an unexpected story of everyday life, with unfamiliar lesbian love and unspeakable desire, fearful sickness and dark despair, helpless struggle, divorce, and needed change, with the ultimate gift of discovery and enlightened growth. This is my story of 60 years. It's the story of what I remember—my experiences, my emotions, and my memories— most of which I have seldom shared.

Most recently, when I have revealed some brief highlights of my life, I'm asked many questions with a sincere interest in my sharing every detail. I sometimes feel embarrassed and uncomfortable just thinking about some of the choices I had made. My lesbian love life, while married to my husband, was a deeply hidden secret for over 20 years. I didn't speak about my Multiple Sclerosis because I didn't want to give it a life. I still don't. I've struggled, and I've made adjustments that I would've never expected to make. And now, because I've worked through my life's challenges, I've experienced so much, and I'm ready to share what I've learned.

Not once, not twice but many times, I can remember wanting something, and while working hard to get it, the feedback has been more discouraging than encouraging. I was told not to apply to be a physiotherapist because "there is too much competition." After having been a physiotherapist for years, I was advised not to open my own physiotherapy clinic because "no one would pay for the treatment here in Canada." Even my doctors told me, "Do not open your own clinic; it will be too much work with your disease," and "Do not have children; you will not be able to take care of them." When I finally got the courage to tell my best friends my secrets, after years of being in the closet, they had warned me not to share with anyone that I was a lesbian. They said that it would be too risky, and I would lose the love of my children, my family, and all of my friends. My lawyer assured me that divorce is always nasty, and ends in constant fighting. Another dear friend said, "You can't have everything you want, so quit being so happy and positive to think that you can."

I can successfully work around and through my challenges. I'm grateful that I'm working through my journey. I've been told that many people around the world would do anything to switch places with me, stand in my shoes, and live the life that I now live. I sincerely believe this to be true, and can't be more thankful for living my healthy, abundant, and authentic life. I experience tremendous amounts of joy, everyday in my life, because of the unconditional love, loyalty, and dedication of my immediate, blended, and extended family and true friends, from near and far, which I've worked so hard to foster.

I see that my genetic make up, family life, education, hardships, losses, and good and bad times, have been my best teachers, leading me through my journey toward creating true joy and better health. I feel that I have a story that needs to be told. I feel that there are many people who would relate to my story, and who would like to know that they are not alone. While reading my story, I want you to be inspired to live the life you were born to live, and create your own true joy and health.

Be real, and focus on your dreams. Visualize often, to really see them. Work hard to create them. And know, deep in your heart, that anything and everything is possible.

Armenians Striving for the American Dream

It's 1957, during the baby boom generation, and I thought growing up then couldn't be sweeter. I was born the youngest daughter of 3 girls, and I strongly remember always being adored and deeply cared for by my parents and sisters; as a matter of fact, I was for sure the favourite. I should mention that each of my sisters thought they were the favourite too. I was always happy and smiling, and didn't have a care in the world. My father, born in Istanbul, Turkey, in 1923, was of Armenian decent. At the age of 19, he was told he had to join the Turkish army. My grandmother, being frantically afraid to lose her eldest son to war, strapped a money belt to my father's waist band, and sent him on his own to the United States of America. He immigrated to the USA, and earned his university degree in engineering, with the ambition of climbing the corporate ladder in order to provide a good life for his family.

Typical of the 1950s, my father worked hard each day, and was home by six o'clock, while my mother happily stayed home to cook, clean, shop, and care for us. I always saw my parents as loving, loyal, and caring, and I always wanted to be just like them, and to follow in their footsteps. As a child, I had never realized what an abundant life I had. I thought I was just like everyone else that I saw, and I thought every family was just like mine. I do remember my mother once saying that when she was growing up in the 1920s and 30s, she didn't have much money, or many things, but her family wasn't poor. Happily, they did their best with what they had. I had always felt like I had more than enough, and I thought that I had the exact same things that everyone else had.

I was born in Detroit, Michigan, a diverse city, yet I can't remember being aware that people had different skin colour, or that people were liked or not liked because of their religion, or where they were born, or because they were different looking. If it was talked about, I didn't place much importance on it. By the time I was 7, we were moving to my third home, and school number 3, in Philadelphia. Going to school, playing with friends, watching *Leave it to Beaver* and *Flipper* on TV, and having family dinners around the table was my daily routine in the 1960s. I always knew that one day, I would be like everyone else that I saw, and go to college, have a good job, get married to a handsome man, and have 3 children. That's what the friends and families I knew did, and I would do the same because that's what I was expected to do, and so that's what I would do to be happy. The life I knew was easy when I did what I thought I was supposed to do.

We really did move a lot. My father would choose to change companies often, in order to get a more interesting, higher paying job with more responsibility. Up until I was 20 years old, I was moving to a new city, a new home, and a new school, with new friends every 2 to 4 years. From Michigan, we moved to King of Prussia, Pennsylvania, right outside of Philadelphia. I loved the apartment-living lifestyle: daily swimming with lessons, sporting competitions, barbecue parties, a playground, and close neighbours to play with, while having the independence to be out and about all day long. Since we often lived in apartments, I was quickly exposed to many people of varied backgrounds. I remember liking everyone, and kept myself busy while helping the lifeguard to clean the pool and organize the deck chairs, helping neighbours carry their groceries into the elevator, and keeping the doorman, Stanley, company at the front desk. My weekly allowance, in 1965, was 10 cents for taking the garbage bags to the incinerator. When it was time to move again, I helped my mother pack up many books, dishes, and trinkets, and I helped my father label and organize the boxes. I kept doing what I was asked to do, and was pleased to do so when it made my parents happy. I liked helping, and seeing people happy. It would be almost a full day before the moving van was all packed up and I would say goodbye to my friends. We'd then be on our way again. Bye, bye.

Moving From City to City to City to City

Saying goodbye to neighbours, friends at school, or even best friends, seemed to come naturally, as I moved far away, over and over again. We would all promise to write and keep in touch, and, in fact, we did. I did the work to keep the relationships alive. I cared about many of them, and keeping a connected link maintained our bonds. Friendships would begin, and as the relationship grew stronger with time, there would be a sudden halt, and it would be time to move. To this day, I continue to work to maintain my childhood friendships, though we may live far apart.

When my eldest sister, Wendy, was 17 years old (I was 8), she began to experience intense knee pain and swelling. She was told by the doctors that she must have injured it while dancing. As her knee pain worsened, she was unable to walk, and she became very ill. In less than one year, my sister was diagnosed with osteogenic sarcoma, and tragically had to have her leg amputated at the hip; she needed to walk with crutches and use a wheelchair. I don't remember a lot of sickness, upset, or sadness from either of my sisters or my parents at that time, although I can only imagine now how sad and upset they must have been.

I suppose my parents may have intentionally hid their feelings, or maintained a sense of calm for the rest of us. Perhaps they were simply grateful that she was still alive, or perhaps they were of the mind, as we would say today, "it is what it is." They seemed to just do their best and move on. Or, maybe, I was too busy playing outside with my matchbox cars, trucks, and friends to notice their upset, or to be upset myself. I do remember fetching crutches, a glass of water, or other things, so Wendy could sit and rest. I also know that she dropped out of college, and would often have to go for physical therapy. When my family was again packing up, this time to move to Toronto, Canada, Wendy independently decided to move on her own to New York City. Only much later did I appreciate just how brave my sister was to move to a place she had never lived, at the young age of 19, after being diagnosed with cancer and losing her leg, and facing all the challenges that were ahead of her.

From Philadelphia, we (minus my eldest sister who was in NYC) moved to an apartment in Toronto, Canada. The phonebook was always my father's link to the Armenian community. While leafing through each page, he would make cold calls to connect with Armenians. He once found his childhood classmate from Istanbul, Turkey, and our families became immediate friends. We joined the Armenian Church as a way to stay connected to Armenian family values and traditions. Surprisingly, after having lived in Canada for only 2 years, I was one of 10 students from the entire school chosen to go on a one-month exchange trip across Canada, representing the *typical Ontario student.* For a school fundraising challenge, I sold the most hot cross buns in a door-to-door sales blitz to earn my $80.00, which would cover the cost of my trip. I learned all the Ontario songs, and blended in quickly and easily. I tried hard at school, and loved spending time with my friends, despite the fact that some of my friends were taking illegal drugs, having sexual relationships (we were 14 years old), and getting into trouble with the law. I somehow seemed to know better, and avoided getting involved.

After enjoying solid friendships for four long years, it was time to say goodbye to Toronto. This move was different; I didn't want to move away, and my sadness got the best of me. For the first time, the tears wouldn't stop. The farewell hugs with my close girlfriends were emotional, and the separation, as I turned to walk away, was heart wrenching. I thought it was unfair, and I was so sad. Perhaps it was my maturity. My relationships with my girlfriends had become important. We had shared many experiences that involved caring, cooperation, and loyalty. I think I now understand that I had learned at a very young age to block out the sad feelings of loss and recurring separation, even though this time it was somehow different. I absolutely did not want to move. When my father asked me if I wanted to keep a Canadian $2.00 bill as a memento, I quickly said no because I was far too sad, and I knew that I would never, ever return to Toronto again.

Now, looking back, I remember feeling so sad, but it didn't linger. I knew there was no other choice. I stayed strong in keeping pace with my parents, and remained positive.

Bumps Along the Way

We moved, this time, to an old, inner city apartment in Queens, New York. Fortunately, we were closer to my eldest sister, Wendy, who had found her stride, and was managing just fine in such a short time. Unfortunately, it was here where I saw my mother suffer her saddest years, languishing while my father was in between jobs and searching for our next place to live. For the first time, I saw my mother cry with worry, often. Sitting together, my mother and I watched TV alone each night while my father travelled around searching for a better job. For the first time, I began to feel her worry, and this scared me. This could be serious; I had never seen her so troubled, tearful, and upset. Feeling her grief, I was now upset, and hated living amongst crowded rows and rows of 10-story brown and red brick apartment buildings that seemed busy and impersonal. I would pray every night that my father would find a job in a new city so we could just leave. I've never realized, until now, how my mother's emotions had influenced my thoughts, and my own anxious feelings and negative perceptions during that short period. She didn't show me that side of her ever, and thankfully, within 3 months, we were moving again. I welcomed the tedious but familiar work to pack up all of our belongings again and move—this time, just outside of Pittsburgh, Pennsylvania—to a beautiful, suburban apartment, surrounded by rolling hills and mature trees, and best of all, I was excited to see children playing on swings, and teenagers on the tennis courts. My prayers had been answered. I was, once again, making new friends at a new school, and involved with more swimming and tennis. I was old enough to get my driver's license at 16 years old, and loved my more grownup freedom. My relationship with my parents throughout my teenage years was always fun, loving, connected, and respectful.

On special days, the students in my school were allowed to take the day off and go to the opening of a Pittsburgh Pirates baseball game. Sitting with my two best friends, we shouted and rooted for our team. I was so excited to be at the game with my classmates, I threw an empty peanut shell down to a friend to get her attention. The peanut shell landed on another girl's sleeve, 3 rows in front of me. She quickly turned around and stood up screaming and swearing at me. Knowing I did nothing wrong, I felt strong, and stood up to this bully; I yelled back, also screaming and swearing. As we were squeezing and pushing our way through the crowded stadium at the end of the ballgame, I was yanked from my two friends, pulled far away from the mobs, and thrown headfirst down to the ground. I was punched, scratched, kicked, and beaten by 5 girls who were clearly looking for a fight. Bruised, bleeding, in pain, and holding broken eyeglasses, I stood up and limped away. I hobbled on the bus, and then stumbled home, feeling upset, hurt, and angry. I walked in the front door, sat at the bottom of the stairs, and began to cry. My mother heard me enter, took one look, sat down, and hugged me. I surely don't remember who won the game, but I did learn the hard way to keep quiet, and ignore crazy, aggressive people.

Remaining in Pittsburgh for only 2 years, we packed up again, and moved to an apartment in Fort Lee, New Jersey. We were within a 15-minute drive to New York City, enjoying frequent visits to see Wendy and her new husband. I was so busy meeting people at school, at community clubs, on sports teams, and during family social gatherings, that connecting to new friends seemed familiar and fun. As a teenager in the 1970s, I grew up only seeing couple relationships between men and women. I was asked about having boyfriends, and was encouraged to dance, date, and go out with boys because one day I would marry one. Then, at the age of 17, I joined in the elegant debutant celebrations at my Armenian Church. I was presented by my father to society, so to speak, and within a year, I ended up falling head over heels in love with my escort, Bob.

I learned to go with the flow, follow the rules, and really appreciate my good friends.

Never Say Never, Ever

Studying physical education at a New Jersey college for 2 years was not really what I wanted to be doing. Yet moving again was not really what I wanted either. In addition to having my own passions for exercise and maintaining my own good health, I also wanted to learn about health, and help other people recover from their injuries and illnesses. Physical therapy seemed to be the profession I was looking for, so another change was imminent. New Jersey didn't have college programs in physical therapy, so the out-of-state application process began. I did all of the research, application filing, and decision making on my own. My relationship with my Armenian boyfriend was now really serious, and we were madly in love, and together all the time. I couldn't wait to play ping pong with him, kiss him, and hug him, and hated to leave him at the end of the day. When he had been accepted, and really wanted to go to a college in Boston, Massachusetts, I decided that I could apply to a physical therapy program at North-Eastern University, another college in Boston, in the hopes that we'd plan our life together. Many people had warned me that being admitted to a physical therapy program was next to impossible, and I should think of alternatives, and not put all of my eggs into one basket.

I applied to five out-of-state physical therapy programs, and kept my fingers crossed. I checked the mail daily in anticipation of my acceptance letters. Days, weeks, and months seemed to drag on until I was accepted to four of the five that I had applied to. I had one rejection: North-Eastern University, in Boston. Devastated, and terribly afraid of the unwanted separation yet again, I realized that I wouldn't be going to Boston with him. I took pleasure in knowing that planning a married life with him would just have to be planned for a little later—just not now. I protected my heart by turning my attention to being overjoyed that I would be studying what I had wanted. Keeping myself from becoming too vulnerable from starting up all on my own, I narrowed my decision to two of the four options. I could continue to live with my parents, and go to New York University, in Manhattan, and be close to family, or go to The University of Toronto, where my other sister, Chris, was living with her husband.

Needless to say, my parents tried desperately to have me stay at home and attend N.Y.U., but they understood when I chose to return to Toronto. My father reminded me that, years before, when we were leaving Toronto, I declined to take the Canadian $2.00 bill, and had said that I would never return to Toronto. I couldn't believe it myself. I smiled as I packed my trunk and suitcases, and was all ready to set out on my own adventure. This time, I was in control of the move, not my parents. This time, it was on my terms. While on one hand it was exciting and exhilarating, on the other hand, I was nervous leaving my family and the latest place I had called home. I would experience my own, new adventure, in a city that I had loved, and would go to a new school, and develop new relationships. Should I say *same old, same old*, or mention that this time, this was now *my* life, and I would make it brand new.

When I'm changing cities again, changing schools again, making new friends again, and having new neighbours again, and leaving friends, neighbours, and stuff behind again, it would make sense for me to refer to my life as "same old, same old." But what the same old routine for me was, again, and again, and again, was a life of frequent change, and my natural ability to easily adapt to the new, where nothing I owned seemed to stay around long enough to save or get old. Nothing was "same old."

Work Hard, Play Hard

Now, back in Toronto, I felt safe and comfortable as I settled into my new home at the university residence, and into a new chapter in my life. I was set up to succeed, by my parents, who had paid for my schooling, room, and board, and two flights home to visit during the holidays. My middle sister, Chris, was a great friend, and gave me strong support as I negotiated my way through my new university life. Immediately, I took part in frosh week (activities at the start of school for the freshman class), and met the most incredible people right away. I tried to follow every rule, be involved in all of the activities, learn what I was taught, study hard to get good grades, and did everything I was expected to do. I had always coloured between the lines, and stayed inside the box, and so far, this had worked for me. The simple follow-the-rules routine kept things uncomplicated and safe for me during the frequent changes.

My first new friend was a physiotherapy classmate, my anatomy lab partner, and we shared a locker that we visited often each day. This was not just by coincidence but because our names followed one another in the alphabet. We both lived in the same residence, and we both had a roommate. Within two weeks of starting class, we requested to switch around our living arrangements with our roommates, so that we could room together, while our roommates would also room together. We designed what we wanted right from the beginning. An instant best friend connection would slowly change my life forever.

Forty hours of class per week meant a lot of prep work, homework, lab work, study time, and exams. She and I did everything together, 24 hours a day. We were almost inseparable, like two peas in a pod, and were so good for each other. I knew from the beginning that She was really smart, and had this photographic memory, which I envied. It was important for us, and most of our friends, to do really well in class, and so it wasn't too difficult to get into the mode of working hard and often, while in class, in the library, and in our dorm. On the other hand, the same friends also liked to have a lot of fun. Together, we would go to parties and dances, and drink wine and beer until the wee hours of the morning. It always seemed like She would be the one to party the hardest, and when it came down to the exams, She would perform the best.

She was so intense, driven, competitive, and so much fun to be with. We would have so much laugh-out-loud, pee-our-pants fun, and at the same time, do really well in school. The only time we weren't together was on the occasional weekend when She would leave to spend time with her boyfriend, who attended another university in a nearby town. During those times, I'd visit my sister, Chris, for dinner, or spend time with other friends living in our residence. While involved with school, I grew apart from Bob in Boston, and we casually ended our relationship. Neither of us had really tried very hard to maintain our connection, so it fizzled. I'm now friends with him on Facebook (of course I am).

Why is the first part of this story helping me to make sense of it all? In the first 20 years of my life, I was lovingly guided to follow my parents' lead to be strong and independent, yet being their child, to do as they wished. I was able to follow society's rules, be respectful, attend to responsibilities, participate in Armenian cultural activities, and build caring relationships, while caring for myself. Were these initial teachings the building blocks for my next 40 years of growth, or would my genetic hardwiring at birth take me to new directions I would have never imagined?

Chapter 2

Loving Him While In Love With Her

Loving Him

During my last year in university, I was more involved and busier than ever. Studying constantly during the day, being president of my class while striving to make a difference, and working 2 jobs at night, took up most of my time, but I always found time to have fun with friends. One night, some friends asked me to join them at the Armenian Church Halloween Party. I hadn't really socialized often with many Armenian friends. The thought of church sounded kind of stuffy, and I didn't have a costume, so I really didn't want to go, but when they insisted, I agreed, and off I went. I knew many of the people at the church, and I was having a pretty good time when I noticed this really nice-looking guy, whom I hadn't seen before. I really wanted to talk to him, but as the night went on, there was no comfortable time for me to approach him. I could've kicked myself for leaving without even asking for his name.

As luck would have it, the next week, the same friend, who I went to the Halloween party with, asked me if I wanted to go to another party, so I decided to join her again. I was absolutely delighted to see the mystery guy from the other party, looking even more handsome than I had remembered. I knew that this time I would make sure to meet him, and I certainly did. We talked and laughed, and shared, for the entire night. When the party was ending, I was absolutely thrilled when he asked if I liked going to hockey games, and then asked for my telephone number. After just meeting him once, he seemed like he was everything I wanted. I saw a nice, really good-looking Armenian guy, with great style. He wore black leather Italian-looking shoes, and carried a black, man purse/bag over his shoulder. Many of my Armenian friends had known him for years, and said he was from a good family. Within the first few months of knowing Him, I got excited when he called me, and thought he was absolutely terrific. After all, in addition to baby blue eyes and a genuine smile, he seemed kind, generous, and smart, and he had a good job, and drove a fancy fast car. What more could I ask for? I was inexperienced and still young, but I liked what I saw.

The 3 years flew by, and graduation day came so fast. I was now a physiotherapist. My parents came from New Jersey, and my entire family attended the graduation ceremony. I was so delighted that He came too, and the look on his face told me that he couldn't have been happier for me, and to be with me. I was ecstatic and so excited to introduce Him to my parents. It was a gorgeous, hot sunny day in June, and each and every one of us were absolutely beaming with joy. She was, of course, there too, and we were all taking lots of pictures while dancing around and hugging each other's family and friends. While I was very proud to have graduated with honours, She had graduated at the top of our class. I had known from the beginning that she was smart, but she surprised us all when receiving the top honour. It was truly the best day, and one that will remain deep in my memories.

Nervous about sharing my news, I figured it was time that I mention to my parents that I was thinking of staying and working in Toronto. My father immediately said that it was time for me to come home because I could easily get a job in New Jersey, and that is where I belonged. Despite a very long and painful conversation, I was unable to convince my parents that I should stay. After arduous attempts to no avail, I agonizingly said a loving goodbye to Him, to Chris, to Her, and to the rest of my friends, and once again... with a very familiar, painfully lonely feeling, I got into the car and peered out of the back window as we drove away.

Saying goodbye again. I felt sadly alone again, and I didn't want to start all over again.

The Perfect Husband, Forever After

I missed Him so much, and He missed me. He would fly to New Jersey to visit me every few weeks. My best friend and I missed each other too, so She drove down with her boyfriend for a visit. All summer, I had friends from Toronto coming to visit, until one day, He asked me to return to Toronto so we could spend more time together. Neither of us were ready for marriage, having known each other for less than a year, but we both wanted to be together, with the thought that we would one day get married. I had long conversations with my parents about moving to Toronto, but they were very adamant and dead against me leaving. For two months, I spoke with them, but they wouldn't budge, and became angry when I just brought up the topic of moving. It was even harder to convince them when my application as a physical therapist, at Hackensack Hospital, in New Jersey, was accepted. I really didn't want to work there when my heart wanted to move to Toronto.

Repeated conversations with my parents ended in the same way. They didn't want me to move to Toronto and follow this man. They thought that if the relationship was serious, then we should be married, and if it wasn't, then I should start my life in New Jersey. I reminded them that He was Armenian, and was kind, generous, and loving, and everything I wanted in a man, but we were just not quite ready to be married. The conversations continued, and my parents' opinions didn't change. The arguments and disagreements would turn to anger. My parents' arguments were hurtful and illogical, and I was feeling so unheard and misunderstood. I felt that at 22 years old, I was not being unreasonable. I was going to ask for their blessing one more time, and then say that I was gong to move. After all, my sister, Chris, was living in Toronto, so at least their visits to Toronto could result in a visit to the two of us. This information made them even angrier, and they resented ever having moved to Canada; they blamed Canada for taking their two daughters. Finally, I begged them to please give me their blessing because I planned on moving to Toronto.

I was about to move yet again. He came to help me pack my few suitcases and drive me to Toronto. I was so confident that I was doing the right thing by moving back to Toronto, that I put on my comfortable *moving away invisible armour* that had protected me in the past. I felt my lips quiver, as I knew I was separating myself from my parents. I stayed strong, and I needed to continue since this was a move I had to do for me.

In the beginning, I lived with Chris and my brother-in-law, who helped me tremendously while I was looking for a job, and an apartment to rent. My parents were so sad and upset for months, that they would call my sister but wouldn't speak with me. I was absolutely devastated when months passed and I hadn't spoken with my parents, who I was so used to connecting with on a weekly basis. *He* knew that I missed speaking with my parents, and hated that they were so upset. He and I thought it best if we got married in six months to appease my parents and, of course, because we loved each other. It made a world of difference to me when my father's spirit improved as soon as we told him that we were going to get married. In the meantime, I was able to secure a full time job at a teaching hospital, and rented an adorable bachelor apartment near Chris's home. I was now becoming settled, relaxed, and really pleased with the way my life was unfolding.

It seemed like most of my friends were getting married, and all at the same time, so we were excited to be sharing in the planning of our lives. I was delighted when She asked me to be a bridesmaid at her wedding. It was to be a fancy wedding with a lot of people. All the bridesmaids had to be fitted for our lovely chiffon dresses. The whole process was such fun. She was delighted to share in the planning of mine too. The thought of getting married was so exciting. He and I planned a small wedding that would be near my family in New York City. We had both dreamed of getting married, and often talked about having kids. I was working, planning for my wedding with him, and planning our life together. At the same time, I often visited with Her, and got excited and chatted about wedding plans and married life whenever we had the chance. My wedding was to be in the Armenian Cathedral, in NYC, with my friends and family in attendance from Toronto and all around the world. I remember my tears of joy streaming down my cheeks as I said, "I do." Nothing could have been better than a long weekend in NYC, to marry the perfect man of my dreams, with visions of happily ever after.

Deeply In Love with Her, Wait What?

I was a happily married woman, with a full time professional job and a wonderful group of solid friendships. I built my life together with Him, loved working hard and long hours to build a career, socialized with family and friends, and took time to visit with my best friend. I visited, laughed, and connected with my girlfriend, often. A perfect, happy life painted the perfect picture.

Then, *this* happened, when I wasn't paying attention. My heart bulldozed toward an unknown, unexpected passion that made my head spin. My double life began:

- romantic candlelight dinners with Him/intense, connected, conversations with Her
- He was loving, attentive, and handsome/She was so smart, exciting, and free-spirited
- stable, familiar city life with Him/active, unfamiliar cottage life with Her
- I learned so much from Him/I learned different things from Her
- family times, with Him, were spent with the church community, backyard parties, and familiar traditions/ girlfriend times with

Her were full of sporting activities, soulful conversation, and new experiences

Marriage is what I had always dreamed of: this beautiful life just like my parents had. Yet while spending time with Her, I felt a freshness, and a freedom, and She totally balanced and completed me. It was an unfamiliar place I had never seen before, but where I felt I was meant to be; and this place had no name—it was a feeling. When She and I were together, the feelings of connection, pleasure, and enjoyment were different than at any other times when I felt happiness. The excitement that I felt when I was planning to see Her, or was with her, took my breath away, leaving me wondering what was happening to me. Why was I feeling this way? We talked for hours about our *special friendship*. Of course, it was special; we had been schoolmates, roommates, and best friends for years. Our relationship felt so familiar and natural, yet we didn't understand the power with which it overtook our emotions. We had fallen deeply and completely in love. We didn't know what to think, but at the same time, I knew that I shouldn't tell anyone or talk about our love with anyone.

How could I love a woman? Could I actually have a loving and intimate relationship with Her? I wanted to. I was feeling guilty having this love with Her, but it was so different than my love for Him. It was the early 1980's, and I was confused, not understanding the meaning of my feelings, and certainly not even considering terms like homosexuality, gay, or lesbian. I just knew I wanted and needed this relationship. I wanted Her. I didn't want to be gay, and I didn't think I was gay, and I didn't want anyone to think I was gay. I knew that being gay was sinning. So, I kept my true feelings to myself, and only showed others my "best friend relationship" that I had with Her. Then, one day, we revealed our feelings of love for one another. Our connected intimacy completely sur-prised us both, and yet the experience was one that we didn't want to ignore, forget, change, or stop. It felt so good and so natural, and so right.

As She became my lover and my best friend/soul mate, our

time together became magical. We would schedule times to be alone together so that nothing else mattered. We cherished shopping together, having meals together, and doing anything just so that we could be close to one another. When I was spending time with Her, I was totally consumed with her presence; her sparkling smile, her scent, her love, her laughter, and the completeness of how she made me feel.

It always felt so right—nothing could have been more right—and still I was puzzled, and sometimes felt so guilty for wanting and loving Her so much. I had never felt like this before. I couldn't get her out of my thoughts or my heart.

Family Times with Him, Private Times with Her

Living with His connecting, unconditional love, while feeling the compelling desire and need for Her, mystified, excited, and upset me. I would honestly love Him, and show my love to him, and secretly hide my overwhelming love for Her. I would openly give my couple time and attention to Him, and secretly give private time and attention to Her. The connections were so different, but I would place Him and Her into separate compartments in my heart, in order to help settle and calm my unexplained need to have Her. I didn't know why I loved her so much, and I didn't know what to do for the preservation of my feelings, and the marriage commitment I had for my husband. So, I didn't think about the conflict in my heart. I went forward in protection mode, and went through my day from one moment to the next.

Life activities became routine and somewhat easy, despite the complexities of the big picture story. Work fell into place nicely, with regular hours and frequent get-away holidays. Caring get-togethers with my family and in-laws seemed to occur quite regularly. Socializing with church friends, work friends, and school friends, helped me keep connected to Him and Her. As our lives became busier, She and I would see each other less often but would find time to get together when we could. I adored her husband, and would look forward to going to their house for dinner, where we would all enjoy one another's company. How crazy as I write this to see how ridiculous this whole scenario was. At the time, I loved my marriage to Him, yet I couldn't wait to see Her, even if it was while visiting with our husbands. I was never jealous of Her husband's love for her, or Her love for her husband. I wasn't bothered knowing that She was making love with her husband, and I enjoyed making love with mine. I felt like this was my life, and there were no options or possibilities for change. It never occurred to me that there might be alternatives to how I was living my life. I had to figure out what to do to function. I planned on staying happily married to Him, and happily loving Her.

When She and I went on skiing trips together, my mother would ask, "Why are you going with Her?" and I would reply that He doesn't really ski, and we would be going on a different vacation at another time, and my mother would say, "Oh, OK, honey," and He and I would go at another time and enjoy one another. When She and I would be going to the cottage, my mother would ask, "Why are you going with Her?" I would reply that he doesn't really enjoy a beach vacation, and we would be going on a different vacation at another time, and my mother would say, "Oh, OK, honey," and He and I would go away and have a great time. Best girl friends traveling together was common, and my parents adored Her; who wouldn't?

My life with Him was very full. Our old friendships became stronger, and new friendships popped up all over. He and I bonded and grew closer together as our relationship passed through the first few years of marital adjustment. I was happy, and I thought he was happy, so I did my best to be a good wife and his best friend. My life with Her was also stronger, but I often felt increasingly uncomfortable with the concealing stories and feelings of guilt. I really didn't know what to do. I just knew that I needed Her in my life, so I needed to make my plans to see her. Our visits got to the point that it didn't matter where we were or who we were with, just that we somehow managed to be together. I needed to be in Her space.

At this time in my life, I knew certain things, and I knew that I didn't know certain things. What I didn't know was how to deal with the things I didn't understand.

Life by Design

Strengthening my marriage – It was 1984; we had now been married for three years. I enjoyed decorating and taking care of our small, 2-bedroom condominium. He and I had conversations about starting a family in a few years, after we got the travel bug out of our systems. We called our 5-week trip to Europe, our *B.C.* (before children) *vacation.* We had a fantastic holiday, and I loved every minute of my time with Him. We talked about everything, and loved watching TV on the couch, all snuggled up together. We regularly played squash, and we went to hockey and baseball games. I really didn't think of Her when I was with Him. It was when I wasn't with Him, while at work, that I missed Her, and needed to design any plan to be with her.

Planning my career – I had just landed a new, full-time physiotherapy position at another downtown teaching hospital. I was really pleased to see friends that I had known from The University of Toronto. There is something so comforting when you see a familiar face in a new workplace. I will never forget how pleased I felt when, on my first day, as I walked into the cafeteria, one of the physiotherapists approached me and invited me to join her for lunch. It's sometimes the small things that are never forgotten. The job was interesting and very challenging, and I was relieved to see how quickly I gained my confidence when providing unfamiliar treatments, in the burn ward, for the first time. Studying the new protocols, and keeping up with my medical files, night after night, exhausted me, but soon, I was really enjoying the intense care that was required. I was soon teaching as a guest lecturer at the university, on physiotherapy for the burn patient. My hard work ethic continued opening doors to new opportunities and work experiences. My career dreams were falling into place. I could see that if I worked hard toward a specific goal, I could achieve it. I liked the hospital life, but I really had my heart set on owning a physiotherapy practice of my own.

Building my relationships – At the same time, I was taking the time to maintain connections with my university and Armenian friends. I organized the social visits, scheduled the outings, and planned the parties. On the weekends, He arranged the road hockey games with all of our friends, including Her and her husband. We also spent a lot of time with my husband's long-time friend, Joe, from high school. When I used to talk about Joe and his son to my colleague, Beth, she would say that she was interested in meeting Joe, and could I plan an introduction. The introduction resulted in a marriage between the two, with my husband and me marching in their wedding. We also became their adopted son's Godparents. I knew, in the back of my mind, that unconditional friendships meant that good friends were friends who didn't require any kind of payment in return. I would give to them with my love, my time, my knowledge, my services, and so on, and they would appreciate it, and I would need nothing in return. I hoped they would do the same for me in their own way. I aimed at securing good relationships so that I could have good friends for a lifetime, in a city I planned on living in for a long time. My past reminded me that I had never really had close friendships in the same city for a long time because I moved so often. I had it in my mind to make sure I kept these friendships strong, forever and ever.

I was determined to stay the course and figure out a way to design my loving life, day by day. It wasn't until some unexpected occurrences took on a life of their own, and threw me right off course.

Keeping Secrets, A Private Love

Putting love and energy into my marriage, working and studying hard to build my career, and taking time to strengthen my friendships were things that came easy to me. I had seen my family designing their lives. I repeated what was familiar, what I had learned, and what I knew. These were the lessons I was taught, and I had practiced them over and over. My mother and father had had a great marriage, and I copied them. Nothing seemed to be a surprise during my regular daily activities.

I awkwardly stumbled when I didn't understand my feelings for Her. Adding the unexpected, unknown passionate love of my girlfriend, tripped me, time and time again. This love was so arousing, exciting, and thrilling, and yet somehow so comfortable, calm, and natural. When we were together, She made my heart fill with delight. I felt like we just fit so perfectly together—a feeling today I still can't explain. And, at the same time, my worry of this unknown place was so painful and confusing, that it caused a profound fear of what this feeling meant. I knew I couldn't be gay, and lesbian was certainly a word I didn't use. I had 1 gay friend from school, and I wasn't like him. I hadn't known any gay female friends, although the class suspected that one of our teachers was gay, but I was nothing like her either.

She always said to me that she was not gay, and that she just loved me. She also loved her husband very much, and she repeated that she would always stay with him. I didn't feel like She had the same fears that I did. I tried to stop thinking about what to call my feelings, and just blindly continued loving Her, and for the most part, I could. But I was married, and I knew our intimate relationship was wrong. I felt like I was between a rock and a hard place, with nowhere to turn for guidance. To me, this feeling didn't have a name, and I continued to feel like I should just keep my thoughts and feelings to myself. I didn't need to talk about it, and no one would know. Who was looking anyways? I suppose a part of me put my head in the sand and ignored the fear and guilt, and I only wanted to appreciate and embrace the love.

So, my day-to-day activities continued as usual. Throughout my days, I would show Him that I loved him, because I did. And I would show my friends and family that She was my best friend, and I loved being with Her, because I did. We went though our days, happily married to our husbands, and living a regular married life, most of the time.

When I was on my own with Her, I was so in love, and then, for just a moment, I would feel the fear of being gay, and felt the guilt of lying and keeping secrets. I didn't understand what was meant by being gay. I had only heard that it was wrong, and a sin. Slowly, these negative feelings would go away because I was so desperate to be with Her behind closed doors. The times together got difficult, especially when I just wanted to touch her or hold her hand, and there was no place to be alone together. Loving Her felt so good, so right, that I thought that it could not, or should not, be wrong. It was an essential, basic part of me, for without this love, I felt I couldn't go on. I had no one to talk to. I had so many questions, and so few answers, so I kept sadly silent.

I guarded my concealed thoughts, private activities, and reserved affection. My secret was unknowingly festering inside me. I would soon see and feel the damage and dis-ease that was taking place deep inside of me.

Chapter 3

1984 with Multiple Sclerosis

OH MY G-D

My *regular life* continued, so I thought. I enjoyed my days going off to work, and coming home to Him for dinner, or spending devoted time with family and friends. On my days off, She and I would get together for a shopping day, or to spend private time alone. This special time was uniquely precious, as it completely blocked out the world around me. My thoughts and feelings were so consumed with Her love, that my entire focus was all about the enjoyment of our time together and how I felt in her arms. Hours would pass in our out-of-this-world place of laughter, connection, and pleasure, until it was time to go home. At the end of the day, I would return to Him, and the previous few hours would totally disappear from my existence, as my *regular life* resumed. I would prepare dinner, and I would thoroughly enjoy my time with Him. There was a point where there were no awkward or doubtful feelings between my very different experiences. I thought that my time with Her was ideal, and my time with Him was ideal, and they both represented meaningful and necessary parts of my life. This sounds awful as I repeat this now, but at that time, I moved from one experience to another, just as you would go from work to home, or to go from family to friends. My emotions were so compartment-alized that I was able to rationalize my relationships as distinct and separate, and necessary. I had no experience in understanding my relationship with Her, so I unintentionally made up my own meanings, and maintained my loyalties to all those around me, the best and only way I knew how.

Life was good, until one day when I picked up the telephone to listen with my left ear, and wondered what was wrong with the telephone. The dial tone was faint, with a very low pitch. When put to my right ear, I heard the dial tone loud and clear. I didn't have any pain in my ear. I hadn't had a cold or sore throat, and I was feeling just fine. I tried to listen to other sounds, and noticed a marked difference between the hearing in my left ear and right ear. Thinking this was quite peculiar, and being curious, I went to the Medical Sciences Library to look up as much information as I could about hearing disorders. I spent hours reading about everything from blockages by wax, to benign tumours, to life threatening diseases. I wasn't too concerned until one day, while sitting at a restaurant with friends, I started experiencing tingles, vibrations, and sensations in my legs and feet, which I had never felt before. Breaking into a cold sweat, I quietly excused myself to go to the washroom. Completely overwhelmed with uncertainty and fear, I stood propped up against the wall while feeling my heart pounding against my chest. I assured myself that I was going to be just fine, turned myself around, and walked back to the dinner table. I wouldn't breathe a word of this to anyone, mostly because I had no idea myself what was happening. Somehow (maybe naive at the time), I knew that if I ignored this, it might go away. Drawing no attention to myself for the rest of the night helped me to return home without mentioning my discomfort to anyone. I went to work, trying to be as normal as possible, the next day. Being normal was hard since I noticed the hearing loss more profound and more often, while the abnormal feelings in my feet and legs began to terrify me. I wondered if anyone could tell that I felt awful. Within a few days, I started to experience blurred, spotty vision, and for the first time, I had a sudden sense of panic and urgency to understand what was happening. I thought perhaps these symptoms could be stress related, although I couldn't put my finger on anything in particular I would be stressed about. When all of the symptoms began to worsen, I really started to panic, and knew that it was time to make a call. OH, PLEASE HELP ME!

Stunned with Disbelief

The next day, I immediately made a doctor's appointment and, thankfully, I was quickly referred to a neurologist at the hospital where I worked. During the next few days, my vision became blurry and spotty, with intermittent foggy patches that worried me more and more. For over a week, I participated in a series of comprehensive neurological assessments, a sequence of inner ear tests, and an eye exam. I was able to take the tests before work started and, at the end of the day, when I had finished treating my patients. To calm myself, I concluded, I probably had an eye or ear infection. At the end of the week, I was called by the neurologist's office, and was told to pick up another requisition for a CT scan. The receptionist handed me the requisition, and on it was written, *CT scan of the head, [Query: M.S.].*

I remember reading the doctors requisition to go for testing, and knowing, or at least hoping, that there had been a mistake, or some wording error. It made no sense that *Query M.S.* was written on the form. A nauseating heaviness tightened my chest, and I felt my face heat up, and my thoughts become confused with scepticism. I laughed to myself out of nervousness. I thought, *no really, this is ridiculous and has to be wrong.*

The CT scan was performed at midnight in the hospital. I drove to the hospital on my own, and I felt like I was in a horror movie, or a really mean nightmare. Following the CT scan, I then had to wait a very slow week to hear from the doctor. I went to the hospital to speak with my new neurologist, who was known to be the best for patients with Multiple Sclerosis. The resident started with a history taking, and then continued with a physical assessment. He had the hearing and vision test reports and the CT scan result. I felt quite good physically, and was calm emotionally, but the whole experience wasn't making sense to me, and I felt my heart rate race erratically. Oh great, now I was having cardiac symptoms.

I wasn't really bothered that my hearing was dull and my vision was foggy. I was focused and concentrating on receiving the CT scan results. After an hour, the chief neurologist entered the office and sat next to me. He read the CT scan results out loud. To this day, I don't accurately remember the exact words. I do remember that he said something like, *"there was evidence of multiple areas of plaque distributed throughout your frontal lobes."* He then confirmed that I had multiple sclerosis. I don't remember if I was alone, or if I went with my husband, or how I felt. I do remember that the neurologist spent time with me reviewing what I should and should not do while knowing that I have M.S. A lot of information was given in a short time, and most of it didn't register at all, except for one instruction.

The neurologist had known that I was planning on having children, and opening a physiotherapy practice. He said—and I do remember this—"Do not have children, and do not open a physiotherapy practice." He went on to explain that, given the signs, symptoms, and diagnosis, the future is unknown, and it would be safer not to take the chances with big responsibilities. While I listened politely, I thought, *Fuck You!* I planned on continuing with my lifelong dreams; that's for sure. Without hesitation or deliberation, my husband and I had a conversation, and decided that we would have children. He said he would rather have our children, and figure out what to do later, while at least we would have the children we had both wanted. We also agreed together that I could plan on opening a physiotherapy practice.

My inner strength was not conscious. It was fuelled by an inner peace and secure knowing that I was going to do my best, and I truly believed that I would be fine.

10 Priorities for Health

1. Joy is a Choice: We are all born with an innate character that comes easy to us. My thoughts, feelings, and things I say and do revolve around being happy. There is little work involved in my being happy. Even when I'm experiencing health challenges, I find good things to see, and reasons to be grateful. My focus is on positive thoughts all of the time. I choose joy.

2. Just be well: I decided early on that I would only tell very close family and friends that I was experiencing health challenges. When I was asked by my neurologist to participate in a support group at the hospital, with others having similar health issues, I declined. I didn't want to think about or talk about anything other than happy thoughts and health. I wasn't going to include this diagnosis into my thoughts, my actions, my body, or my life story.

3. Focus on what makes sense: I was so pleased, and felt very relieved when my husband was encouraging about having a family, and supported me on my plan to open a physiotherapy clinic. I knew that we would be a strong team, and I needed his love and care. When thinking of the diagnosis, I considered telling Her that I couldn't continue with our relationship because I needed to dedicate my time and energy to my health and my husband. I would feel so anxious when thinking to tell Her, but I was so afraid for my health. I needed to live a typical life, and put away the new and unknown feelings that I didn't understand. Being gay was difficult, and these feelings occupied too much thought and emotion. My health could be fragile, and I couldn't take any chances of weakening it. I tried to stay strong, but I was troubled, and had to think about this long and hard. I searched for common sense answers that I found difficult to find.

4. Eat to Live: Eating healthy, starts with discipline. I'm grateful for another character trait that came easy. I've enjoyed healthy food, and I've just stuck to whole real foods in moderation, no matter what.

5. If you can, you must: As a physiotherapist, I've lived an active lifestyle when at work, in my leisure, and especially at my laziest times, because I must continue to be active here and now, while I can. I've always known that exercise is the best medicine to stay healthy, mentally and physically.

6. Only show true love: I always felt that if I gave love all of the time, then love would come back to me. True love is healthy when there's no guilt.

7. Have dreams: When I first heard the diagnosis of M.S., I created vivid dreams of healthy children, a loving family, and a successful physiotherapy practice. I saw it, and as each day went by, I imagined the dreams coming true.

8. Work on goals: I made long lists of things I had to do. I realized early on, while providing physiotherapy, that there are many ways to promote healing and maintain health. Effort had to be put on every priority to realize the results.

9. Try hard: I always tried my best. I often felt like a dark, weighted cloud had been put over my head and shoulders. It was harder for me to focus on moving forward when I noticed that my loss of hearing and eyesight was getting in my way. I still remained positive.

10. Be grateful: Each day that passed, I'd be so relieved that my symptoms weren't getting worse. When feeling grateful, I would feel better. Every single day, I would give thanks that I was feeling better than the day before. Every day, I said, "Thank you. Thank you for my health; I feel good." Every day, I felt better.

Joy can be a choice; health will follow joy. Choose joy; think health—create each day.

It's a Girl – Dreams Come True

I told my entire family, but very few friends, about my symptoms and the diagnostic tests that confirmed I had M.S. I kept rather quiet about the M.S., to keep it quiet. I did share with my family that the neurologist had advised me not to have children, and not to open a physiotherapy practice. Of course, they were all very shocked, and told me how concerned they were. I, too, was concerned but not afraid, and assured them that I was doing my best to stay healthy. Then, I strongly and proudly announced, with a radiant smile on my face, that my husband and I planned on having children soon, and I was going to open a clinic. With my focus in place to concentrate on being healthy, I was really excited about the thought of having children and a physiotherapy practice.

I imagined myself opening a clinic but wondered where it should be. My husband and I went house hunting, and drove to one of our favourite neighbourhoods, wanting to buy a house where we would raise our children. I planned to open a clinic in my home, so this home needed to be suitable for receiving patients in the lower level. I remember saying that I wanted a house on a certain street because it was within walking distance to public transportation, and was close to parks and shopping. When driving on that street, there was a house for sale, and it had the perfect setup as a home/clinic. We both loved it, and on my 28th birthday, we put in the offer; when everything was said and done, we bought it. In that moment, I again felt so grateful. I couldn't wait to share the news with my family, and with Her. I loved sharing news with Her; I could almost see her smile, and could sense her happiness, every time I shared my moments of joy.

What a blessing when I got pregnant right away. Everything just kept getting better. My due date was December 27, 1985, and I was anticipating the best Christmas ever. I had heard that women with M.S. often feel better with pregnancy. And sure enough, as time went on, my eye site began to clear, and my hearing improved. The odd tingling feelings in my feet were disappearing, and I was feeling a little stronger and more balanced. My belly was getting bigger, my spirits were high, and I felt healthier than ever. Although I was noticing my health continuing to improve everyday, I still had the fears of the diagnosis lingering in the back of my mind.

I continued to take care of my home, and I still spent time with Her, as well as a lot of time with my husband and our families. I worked right up until one week before Christmas. On December 27, 1985, I went into labour, right on schedule. The doctors suggested that I not have an epidural because of my history of M.S. I hadn't considered having a natural childbirth, but at that time, there were no choices. After hours of painful labour, with lots of pushing and deep breathing, with my husband close by my side, our healthy daughter, Nicole, was born. She was immediately placed on my belly, and I felt my living miracle cuddled up in my embrace. That same night, I remember being very alert and quite mobile, not having had the epidural. Things got even better when She and her husband came to the hospital that night to surprise us, and celebrate with tiny appetizers and a bottle of champagne. I had a blissful nights sleep.

This small black cloud constantly hovering over me has always created an insecure uncertainty as to what may be in my tomorrow. I know I'm so fortunate to be as healthy as I am. Is this partially luck? I must keep dreaming and imagining, and doing what I'm doing. Thinking positive thoughts, and seeing the good all around me, works for me. Still choosing joy. Still focusing on health.

Mom's Struggles with Cancer

Caring for a new baby and renovating a new house, during uncertain times, was a challenge to say the least. But I was on maternity leave for the following year, so I knew it would be possible. It was also a good time to begin the planning for my clinic.

I certainly had my work cut out for me.

One day, during a follow up medical appointment with my neurologist, I shared the details of my new daughter, my new house, and the upcoming plans of my new clinic. My doctor shook his head, and said I was denying my disease, and was too at ease. I watched him write this note in my medical chart, and I smiled inside, not really caring what he wrote. I commented that I didn't think that I was denying the disease. I was continuing to see improvements, so I was feeling better, and I had a positive outlook, choosing to recognize the improvements I was feeling. I walked out of the office without making a follow up appointment. I didn't plan on returning.

Unfortunately, shortly after that visit, I started experiencing very sharp and painful headaches, and was upset when I had to go back to the doctor. I was prescribed Prednisone, a strong corticosteroid drug to ease the pain. I decided to hold off taking it for just a few days, knowing the side effects of the medications. Then, while sitting home one night, my father called from New Jersey, with devastating news. My mother had been diagnosed with stomach cancer, and she was very, very ill. Without delay, I flew to N.J. to spend a week with my mother, leaving Nicole with her dad. I was devastated when I saw that my mother didn't even look like herself. My mom's arms and legs were so very thin, and her belly was bloated. Coincidentally, she too had been taking Prednisone, and had the side effects of a *moon face*, which was a distorting facial swelling. I decided then that I couldn't take the prescription I had been given. Instead, I took some over-the- counter pain pills, and promptly threw the tablets out. Following a week of nurturing my mom, her health stabilized, and I returned home to my family. I soon began to have fewer headaches, and felt relief from the simple over-the-counter medications. Over the next few months, I flew back and forth to New Jersey to spend time with my mom, as her health sadly deteriorated.

In between my visits to New Jersey, I planned and designed my physiotherapy practice. The plans went from opening the small practice in my home, to opening a practice in partnership with my friend, Beth, at a large shopping mall. The two of us had left our jobs at the same time to have our first baby. We had both dreamed of opening a clinic, and our decisions to form a partnership were well-timed. So, the detailed hard work began. It seemed like there was never enough time to organize all of the meetings with the bankers, lawyers, accountants, equipment providers, contractors, and doctors. We would take our babies with us in their strollers from office to office, finalizing the deals. During the many months, there were cancelled meetings and contractor delays, and in between, I would fly to New Jersey to visit with my mom. Thankfully, our passions, communications, and attention to detail during all of the meetings was so flawless that we were able to pull everything together and prepare for the opening of our physiotherapy practice in less than a year. The open house date was set for Monday, August 17, 1987. Invitations were sent out, and we all expected to cut the ribbon, and bring out the bubbly champagne on the Monday.

Then the dire telephone call came to me the Friday before. My father said that I would have to fly to N.J. since my mother was very ill, and may not survive much longer. While sitting alone and peering out of the window seat, I quietly wept during my entire flight home to New Jersey.

R.I.P. Mom 1923–1987

After a long and sleepless two days with my father and sisters, by my mother's side, my mother passed away peacefully. I spent a sad and emotional week with my family, mourning my mother's death. I know that the timing of a death is never right, but this timing was really wrong. She was just 64 years old, and had left all of us way too soon. She had so much more life to live, and I had so much more life to share with her. I had more thoughts that I would have wanted to say, and more about me that I wish she had known. I would love to have known her thoughts and opinions.

My mother had expressed a wish to be buried wearing her wedding band. My father, unable to do it himself, had asked me if I would put her band on her finger before her burial. I felt quite honoured, and was pleased that I was going to have a little more time to say goodbye. In my last moments with my mother, I reached into the casket where she lied so beautifully in her favourite bright red dress, and held her cool but soft hand in mine. I kissed her hand and slipped the golden band onto her finger. I whispered, "I love you mom," and sadly realized that I would have to carry on without her in my life, but knew that she would always be around me, and in my heart-filled memories. I often feel her presence around me, and especially right now.

As soon as I returned to Toronto, I focused my attention on my husband and daughter, and got busy preparing the clinic for welcoming our patients. Keeping busy was a great way to occupy my sad heart. But I was feeling annoyed because there were many unfinished jobs at the clinic. The extra work, when I was tired and had little energy following the funeral, completely frustrated me. I could've taken my time, or not have done some of the work at all, but I felt compelled to finish each and every last detail that I had worked so long and hard to plan. I wanted to impress and wow the patients as they entered the clinic. I remember staying at the clinic, night after night, until the wee hours of the morning, painting, fixing, cleaning, and organizing the filing cabinets, until I was satisfied that everything was presentable.

Working alone was very difficult, and I spent a lot of time overthinking about the meaning behind my mother's passing at the exact same time as when my clinic was to open. My mother had been ill for so long, and I spent a long time preparing for my clinic's opening. Yet the closure of her life, and a brand new opening to a part of my life, came together at the exact same time. This was no coincidence. I was in an emotionally sad state, yet envisioned new, exciting doors opening. At the end of that first week home, when most of the work was done, I sat back exhausted but relieved in the brand new, empty waiting room of my clinic. While gasping a big sigh of satisfaction, I stared for a long time at the reception desk, file cabinets, and entrance to the gym that I had helped to design and construct. My dream had been realized. My mood lifted and strengthened, and I felt so proud. My mother would have been proud too. My clinic was truly open for business.

If it's not one thing, it's another. It was time to address my struggle on whether to continue or not continue with my complicated, yet needed relationship with Her.

It was time to pause and take a deep breath during this intense and stressful phase. The deep sorrow following my mother's death, the excitement yet demanding strain of a brand new clinic, and the responsibility of a one-year-old daughter, needed dedication to my loving husband, and urgency to maximize my own health. The work needed attention, while attempting to close an unexplained emotional need, and frantic desire, to be with "Her."

Chapter 4

Feeling Guilty and Fragile

Hiding in Plain Site

Since my eye site and hearing, and the feelings in my feet and legs, were remarkably getting better, I thought of everything I could do to make sure things continued that way. I couldn't help but notice with the death of my mother, and the newness of my daughter and physiotherapy clinic, that a wide-open space had been created for me to concentrate on this new chapter in my life. From time to time, I still remembered the cautions that the doctor had stressed, and of feeling very guarded and fragile. I didn't take for granted that my good health could change at any moment. Even though I had never read or learned the practice of mindfulness or gratitude, I knew, instinctively, that I had to count my blessings often, every single day. I also clearly saw the good things in my life, the constant love that I felt, and the incredible strength that I had. I remember looking out to the trees, and being grateful that I could see, and listening to the wind, and the birds singing, while quietly celebrating that I could hear their songs. I was determined to eat well, exercise, and take great care of myself. What I didn't like, were the frequent thoughts of guilt when I was deceiving my husband when being with Her. I didn't want to admit to myself that I should spend more time exercising, being with friends, family, and my clinic, and less time with Her. My mind jumped back and forth between replaying the anticipated excitement of being with Her, to the guilty thoughts of not telling Him.

My busy schedule involved a lot of multitasking. I had a regular schedule at my clinic, which allowed my business partner and me to share an au pair to take care of our children at each of our homes. Three days a week, I'd go to the clinic, while the au pair stayed at my home with my daughter. I'd spend more than 12 hours each day, attending to the clerical work, clinical upkeep, treating clients, writing reports, and cleaning up. On my off days, my business partner did similar tasks to keep the clinic running, while our au pair stayed at her home with her son. My husband and I took turns and shared the responsibility of caring for our daughter. I'd make the plans so that we'd also socialize with our friends and family, and spend quality time together. I loved my husband, and really wanted to make sure that we were happy, had fun, and talked through our conflicts. By the time the days were done, I had less time to spend with Her. I was torn between spending loving time with Her, or doing what I thought was best at that time for my health and marriage. She'd ask to visit with me; to be honest, I can't even remember the reasons I gave when I said that I couldn't see her. I do remember, on one occasion, I was feeling weak and tired, and needed to just relax. We had planned on going to the cottage together, and I didn't have the strength or vigour to go, so I cancelled. She encouraged and almost begged me to go, but I just didn't have the stamina; I said no, and didn't go. She was devastated, and I was tired of disappointing her. I couldn't live feeling guilty on so many fronts, and be healthy, with Her in my life. From then on, I chose not to get together with her, and I wanted our closeness to fade. I didn't want to want her, and I didn't want her to want me. My feelings of guilt were becoming too intrusive, and interfered with my naturally happy spirit. I saw Her less and less, until I made myself too busy to visit with her, or even think about her.

I wouldn't find out until years later that while I was focused on moving forward for my own health and the stability of my family,

"She" was left feeling abandoned and absolutely devastated. I never knew. To this day, I'm so sorry that, at that time, I hadn't had the skills, or compassion, or the knowledge to communicate in a way that could have caused "Her," "Him," or me, less pain. There is a lot I am sorry for today.

Choosing Healthy

When Nicole was 3 years old, my husband and I were ready for, and wanting, another child. While I was feeling well, I wanted to do as much as I could, and experience everything. I was at a time in my life when my health was at its best. I was winning again at squash, going on biking and skiing trips, and working hard at the clinic, while spending quality time with my daughter. I wanted to make sure that my neurological health was stable. It was time for me to go for a follow up appointment with a new neurologist. Another CT scan and more examinations would perhaps help me understand the signs that I couldn't see but should see. The information might help with my decision to have another child, even though I chose to have a child before, when I was advised not to. This time, it was different, because I had the added responsibility of another young life, and needed to be there for my husband.

During my visit to the doctor I was told that the CT scan showed that I had signs of plaque throughout my brain. The neurologist said that it looked like a brain filled with white popcorn, which, generally, was not a good sign. He then went on to ask, "How do you feel?" I replied, "I'm great; I'm active, thriving at work, and taking good care of my family." The neurologist said, "Well, then you could proceed to do what you want to do, and have another baby because you feel well, or you can decide not to have the baby because of the results of this test." He went on to say that there are many people who have normal CT scan findings but have mobility impairments and require a wheel chair, and there are people like me who function perfectly but have abnormal test results. With a big, genuine smile, he advised me to do as I wished and have another baby, because what I was doing and how I was feeling was still working for me. He repeated that I could go forward because of test results, or go forward because of how I feel. I left the office feeling really good, and...feeling not so good.

What kept coming into my thoughts and didn't change, was my knowing that I had this diagnosis, and a CT scan that confirmed M.S. I was so grateful when I felt well, and held onto that feeling. I made it a point to appreciate how fortunate I was to be feeling so well. I went from one day to the next, only sharing with people how great I felt. As you can see, I continue expressing how well I feel, still today. When people would ask, "How are you?" as they passed by, I would say, "Great," or "fantastic," or "terrific." Their comments back to me would be "That's so good to hear," even though they didn't know that my health was not perfect, and they really didn't realize how truly happy I was, in comparison to my tests, since my health could have been a whole lot worse.

Another natural childbirth, and healthy daughter number two was born right on time. The second child, or maybe the experienced parents, seem to be much calmer, making things easier. The experience of everyone taking part makes the little jobs that were once difficult, quite routine. After a couple of months, when life seemed to go smoothly, and everything fell nicely into place, I returned to treating my patients. While Nicole was going to the Armenian nursery school, Tania would be at a babysitter's home, or would accompany me to work at the clinic for a few hours.

Through the years, when I've responded with "I'm great," everyone who knows me would say, "You always say you're great." And I know in my heart that that's because I am great. They don't know how grateful I feel. I'm so fortunate to be as healthy as I am— lucky me. I now know that life is not just what happens to me but how I react to it.

Building Strong Bonds for Lasting Relationships

I was fortunate enough to have the flexibility to arrange my day at the clinic to fit my family's wants and needs. From the age of 2 ½, my daughters were able to go to the nursery program at the Armenian school. It was a small school (120 students, ages 2 ½ to 12 years old) that was connected to the Armenian Church. The teachers were caring and devoted to the kids and the community. The parents knew one another, and had close relationships outside of the school. I'd drop my daughters off, three days a week, at 8:00am, and pick them up at 4:00pm, giving them a full day of learning with cultural heritage, and me a full day at the clinic, or running errands. I liked to volunteer as supervisor during school trips, and I was always able to take them to the doctor or dentist, and to their evening activities, like swimming and gymnastics, which I thought was an essential yet cherished job of being a parent. I was free to exercise in the middle of my day, go shopping, or have lunch with my friends, mother-in-law, or husband, who also had a flexible work schedule. My days were filled doing a lot of things with a lot of people.

Our family would go on vacations to the U.S. to visit more family, or go on vacation with friends to experience new places. I really loved being the driver during our road trips. My husband would entertain the kids with his puppet shows, from the front seat, feeding us snacks, while I would be focusing on the road. One year, my good friend and I wanted to surprise our husbands for Valentine's Day. We planned a three-day getaway trip to NYC. I booked the flights, hotels, dinner, and Broadway show reservations, and arranged babysitting for the kids, with other close friends. We had planned this surprise for a couple of months, and I couldn't wait to see the look of surprise on my husband's face. Then, remembering that my husband really didn't like surprises, I told him 2 days before we would go, to give him time to do his own planning. He listened to my news with a joyful smile, and then suddenly his smile faded, and he asked, "But what about the kids?"

I looked back at him and gasped, and replied, "Oh no; Oops, I forgot about the kids!" We both laughed, and after I shared all of the details, my husband relaxed, and was excited to go. I always cherished that NYC Valentine's Day vacation, and the many other great vacations I planned with family and friends. I worked on enhancing my relationships all of the time.

When many more years had passed, my husband and I decided to have our third child. I didn't have to think twice, but I knew that I should go back to the neurologist one more time to get another health check just to make sure. I had physical examinations and MRIs. When the results were in, the story was the same. There were signs of M.S. plaque formation in my brain, and slight physical abnormalities consistent with M.S. Again, I was asked how I felt and how I was doing. My reply again was that I was still playing squash and doing all of the physical activities that I had always done, and I was feeling great. With a steady and strong voice, my doctor told me that I now had the diagnosis of benign M.S. because my signs and symptoms had not changed significantly in the last 10 years. He then commanded me to do as I had been doing because it was still working. I was absolutely delighted to follow his instruction, and went home to announce that we could, and should, have a third child.

It was extremely important to me to build strong, loving, and lasting relationships with friends and family, so I gave my time and caring energy to those important to me, whenever I could. I invested in my friends as a selfish act. I cared for and cherished my friends.

Fireworks at the University Reunion

It was 1990, and time for a 10-year U of T physio reunion. There are those who love reunions, and those that fear or hate them, and never attend. I'm one of the ones who look forward to catching up with my friends, and knowing what they're doing. I thought I would initiate this one, having been the class president. We got together and agreed on who would complete what tasks. I was to call a select group, and speak with them on the telephone to make sure they had received the invitation and emails. My emotions were all over the place when I agreed to call Her. I was very excited, a bit nervous, and even too stressed to make the call, but I wanted to make sure that she would be attending, so I had to. It was my job, after all. I hadn't spoken with her in more than 5 years, having made myself busy with work and the family, and probably a lot of avoidance on my part. I tried hard to stop wanting her. It worked for a while. But I couldn't stop thinking about her. I realized, as a lesbian, I couldn't hide, or hope to turn straight. I began to understand that I was ready to reconnect again, and when putting my fears far away, I realized how much I had missed her, and how excited I was to know that I'd see her again. I was thrilled when she agreed to attend, and we both decided to go on our own without our husbands.

Over 100 people attended. Each mingled around the restaurant, going from person to person, talking, sharing, and laughing, while nibbling and drinking at the different mouth-watering food stations. I said hello, and hugged a lot of friends right away. Then, I saw Her. When she looked at me, my heart totally skipped a beat; then, it was beating so fast, hard and so loud. that I thought that someone would hear it. She looked as adorable as ever. It hadn't been that long, but I guess trying to put Her out of my mind for all those years clouded my memories a bit. I didn't want Her to look so good. I didn't want to want her so much. I had been in such a survival mode to ignore my feelings for her that I had been wearing a very thick shield. I had gotten so good at protecting my heart by building walls around it. As soon as I saw Her, the shield melted away, and I felt weak. I said a timid hello, and shared old stories with our friends, but I felt that there was a big elephant in the room because She and I really hadn't spoken much with one another. We laughed with all of our friends a lot but didn't laugh with each other. Of course, no one had known that we had been lovers. I felt awkward, and she probably felt the same. The atmosphere was happy, and the energy was exciting, and I felt that the evening was a success, but it was not quite finished for me. At the end of the evening, after I had said my good byes to the group, I asked Her to sit with me in my car so that we could catch up some more. I remember that she hesitated, and I had to convince her. We ended up talking for hours about all the good times that we had had. Then She revealed how much pain she had felt when I had stopped calling her. I had figured that she wouldn't have been happy, but I didn't stop to really consider how she was really feeling. I apologized for not knowing how distraught she had been all through the years, or enquiring on how she had been feeling or what she had been doing. I'm sure my lack of inquiry was to protect myself, but that was no excuse.

While we were sitting in my car, I was in love with her all over again, and was reminded of the strong attraction between us. I had tried to stop and forget this feeling, but it was unstoppable. All of the love songs in the world could not have come close to describe the way I was feeling. I knew that this feeling was different than any other feeling of love I had experienced. Well, this time, I was going to be the one to start up the relationship. I had to try. I wanted to be with her all the time. This love was significant, and I was willing to do anything to make it work. I was willing to risk my happy, married lifestyle to spend time with Her. I was in love.

Taking Risks for Unstoppable Love

I had loved my parents, my children, and, of course, my husband, but this love was so very different. I really didn't know what to do with it, but I knew that I desperately needed Her in my life, and I knew it was completely unexplainable, and I didn't care. I had stopped calling Her after many years of being together because I thought it was affecting my health. I felt that my relationship with Her was wrong; I felt ashamed, and thought that my fears when being with her were connected to my failing health. I had needed to focus and concentrate on myself, and my family, and my career goals. Then, again, my desire for being with Her had exploded into a strong devotion that monopolized my thoughts, and I had to be with her. Not being with her was also making me sick—sick to my stomach.

I no longer felt that the love was wrong; it couldn't be wrong. I did all that I could to speak with her on the phone, visit with her at one of our homes, meet for coffee, or go for dinner. We even went to lesbian movies together, even though she still considered herself not to be a lesbian. I was still unsure. We would travel together on vacation, and spend a week being together when we could. Sometimes we'd travel with our kids to the cottage, and I felt like we could have so easily lived together. When I held Her in my arms, I felt the connection. She continued to say that she wasn't a lesbian, and that our love was just love.

I had so many questions, and wanted to learn more; I was searching to understand why I was feeling this way. We had very long talks about our intense feelings, and our needed love. I was always so bothered that I felt so guilty all the time. I didn't want to think that I was gay. There were too many reasons why I didn't want to be gay. If I was gay, I'd have to divorce my husband, and I certainly didn't want to even consider that. If I was gay, I would have to tell my children, and they wouldn't understand. As I matter of fact, I didn't understand, so how I could I expect anyone to understand? So, the questions went unanswered, and I just continued to live, day by day, just praying for the answers to appear.

It was harder for me to separate my emotions when being with Him, and then being with Her. I was no longer good at compartmentalizing my emotions or my daily tasks. I liked myself better, and felt more like me when I was with Her. I'm not sure why, but I just did. I knew things were changing when I only wanted to be with Her and our kids, and I felt empty with Him. It got to the point where I liked Her more, and Him less. When my life became an emotional roller coaster, I had trouble focusing, and I didn't know which way to turn, so I started seeing a psychologist. Week after week, the psychologist asked the questions; I talked and talked, and I'd come up with things to work on. We talked about my husband, my children, my siblings, and my work, and, of course, Her. The conversations quickly focused on how I felt when I considered myself to be a lesbian. The more we discussed me being a lesbian, the more comfortable I got with everything— from me saying it, to learning about it.

I was becoming comfortable learning, and headed off to the self-help books at the stores. I felt a little self-conscious, and constantly looked around to make sure I didn't see anyone I knew. I bought books rather than leave a paper trail at the library, and I'd read them secretly. Then, I'd wrap them up in plastic bags, and throw them out on garbage day so that they wouldn't be discovered. I'd drive up and down the streets of our gay neighbourhood (gaybourhood), wondering who was there. I seemed to only notice those who were poorly dressed, tattooed, and pierced, and were not like me. I saw few people who looked like me. Then, one day, my psychologist gave me a flyer: *Lesbian Support Group – Women married to men, and questioning their sexuality.*

Peeking Out

There had been a shift. I wasn't quite ready to go to the lesbian support group, but I was willing to open up and learn more about the gay world. I was very surprised to read books about married women having relationships with other women, very similar to mine. I'd also read books on lesbian love, and stories about lesbians. It also interested me to read about people feeling gay as a child, or recognizing their feelings later on in life. I read about the gay men and the lesbian women. I had been a tomboy, and enjoyed cars and sports more than dolls and fashion. A lot of women had been tomboys, and not all tomboys are lesbian. I had adored my girlfriends when I was young, and I admired many female actresses and singers, but that didn't confirm anything.

I wanted a script, but as I read more, I learned that I really didn't have to learn anything. What I did know was that I deeply loved a woman. I felt comfortable around Her, and preferred being with her more than with Him. I was only reminded that this was a struggle because I was already married to a man. It was the early 1990s, and the word gay was not such an unknown or forbidden word in Toronto. But chatting about gays, and seeing gay athletes, actors, or politicians, wasn't that common. A conversation about gays around the dinner table, or at a party in my Armenian circles, was rare. If the topic of gay was brought up by someone else, I'd first listen, and if I thought that I could contribute without being too gay positive, I'd add to the conversation. Looking around the table of friends, I could tell who was comfortable and open to conversations about gays, and who definitely wasn't.

I kept a low profile so as not to introduce suspicion or too many questions on why I was so interested. I didn't want to have strong opinions that may lead to anyone thinking that I was gay. I remember one time, during a friend's barbeque dinner party, the topic of gay athletes came up. My friend voiced his opinion that he didn't approve of the gay lifestyle. His adult daughter quickly joined the conversation in support of gays. A rather heated discussion ensued, and I felt so awkward that I decided to keep quiet. When conversations about gays came up, I'd stay out of them so that I wouldn't be discovered. Yes, I was feeling guilty, and I didn't want anyone to discover my secret because I had too much to lose.

Once I began to consider that I was a lesbian (it's like learning a new word, and suddenly you see it and hear it all over the place), I was frequently hearing conversations about gays and lesbians all around me. When my youngest daughter Gabi was to be baptised, my husband and I wanted to select her Godmother. After considering several close family members, we chose his cousin. She was a wonderful lady, and we both loved and admired her tremendously. We thought she'd be a great role model, and she hadn't had children, so we hoped she would welcome being our daughter's Godmother.

When we asked her, she immediately said yes. She also wanted to share with us that she wanted us to know something about her that may influence our decision. She said that she'd feel OK if we decided to change our minds. She then told us that she was a lesbian, and although she didn't talk about it, many people knew. I had to work really hard not to smile. I had a hunch that she was, so I wasn't totally surprised, but thrilled that she would be in our lives. My husband had never been told, but he too wasn't surprised. We both agreed that her being a lesbian didn't change our decision, and we were thrilled that she'd be our daughter's Godmother. The topic of lesbian was getting more comfortable and more familiar in our lives. Oh no, how long could I keep quiet?

Wanting to Speak Out

One relaxed morning, while my husband and I were still in bed, we began talking about Gabi's baptism party plans. I was in a great mood, and so looking forward to our relatives visiting us from the USA and Europe. On the topic of the baptism, I brought up a conversation regarding how delighted I was that his cousin would be our daughter's Godmother. I shared my thoughts on the fact that she had told us that she was homosexual, and I was pleased that neither one of us considered it to change our decision and, in fact, I liked that she was open with us. I remember how I felt when he began to say that although he was all right that she was open, he felt that he didn't like the fact that she was homosexual. He would open up and say that he thought it was wrong. I rebutted, and said that it wasn't wrong. We debated back and forth about homosexuality being an abomination in the bible, and how he believed it wasn't really normal or approved by society. At that time, I was uneducated and not well spoken on the topic, and, in fact, quite lost for words. It was clear to me, however, that he wasn't approving of homosexuality, and I quieted, thinking that it would be a bad time to tell him that I was having trouble with my own feelings. I was looking for ways to drop hints, but this wasn't the right time.

On another occasion, when I could have opened up slightly to share my feelings with Him and my dad, I once again quieted in fear of anger, disapproval, or disappointment. My family was visiting my father in North Carolina, and the kids had gone to bed. My dad, my husband, and I were relaxing in the living room after dinner with our coffee and dessert. My husband asked my dad, somewhat out of the blue, "Dad, how would you feel if one of your daughters was gay?" My father replied, "But they're not," and He said, "But what if they were?" My dad, a politically correct man back then, said, " I'd feel fine; it would be O.K. with me." Needless to say, that I was so surprised that my husband had asked the question, and even more surprised—, but maybe not—, that my dad was so relaxed and nonchalant about the topic. I was certainly relieved that my dad replied that way, and suspected that my husband asked thinking that my dad would reply that he'd be disappointed, or have a less positive response. I think it was that day that I felt that He suspected that I was gay. I so wanted the conversation to continue, but I didn't know how to participate to keep it going. I got tripped by my own shaky nerves, and couldn't find the right words to keep me out of trouble. Quickly, and maybe deliberately, my dad switched the topic to something completely different. Did my dad suspect? I kept my secret once again. I'll never know how he would have really felt; my dad died of cancer later that year, while living in North Carolina.

The longer I stayed in my closet, the harder it was to get out. I looked for opportunities or situations when I could tell Him that I loved Her. When I spoke with Her, she begged that I never tell Him. She once said, "He might become angry and hurt one of us." I assured Her that there were no indications that He would ever hurt anyone. She would say, "Anyone can crack, and our situation is so unusual." I refrained from telling Him because I was afraid of the unknown. Then, when I spoke with my therapist, she asked me why I wanted to tell Him. I repeated, several times, that I wanted to have an open and honest relationship with my husband. She suggested that I get a divorce first, and then, after the divorce is settled, I could go on with my life, and decide to tell him or not. But I said that I didn't want to get a divorce, and I just wanted to be honest. My therapist advised that I give it time. How much time is time, I thought, and what would I learn with more time?

It was so hard to be me without causing sadness and hurt in others. Opinions are often helpful, but in this case, they brought about my anxiety and fears that silenced me again.

Chapter 5

To the E.R: Secrets Can Kill You

Deception for Survival

The strength of the shift got even stronger. I looked forward to being with Her, more and more. We would plan our getaways in the evenings after I was home from work, and the kids were in bed. We would meet at a coffee house, and sit for hours talking, or we'd sit in my car, and talk while listening to music. The feel of Her soft skin, and smell of her perfume, would make me crazy. Just holding hands when in the car would make my pulse race and take my breath away. There were times when I would come home after having been with Her, and my kids would say, you smell like Her. I knew I was in trouble, and I was losing my mind when I would dream of running away with Her to another country, and living happily ever after. But I knew that could never happen.

I still did my best to give it my all when I was at work, and I always got excited when I would take my daughters to school, gymnastics, or swimming. I would look forward to playing squash with friends, or going with our whole family visiting. But the alone time with Him was getting more and more difficult, and I wanted to tell Him, but I couldn't. I didn't want to hurt Him. I had been dealing with my feelings for more than 15 years; how could I expect Him to begin to understand. I didn't know what to say because I didn't have any suitable words that would explain my absurd predicament. I had never had a lesbian friend, and had never known of anyone married, in a heterosexual relationship, who was homosexual.

I looked for opportunities to open up conversations about gay issues with him. I thought an easy and harmless discussion would be to chat with him about his cousin who openly shared with us that she was a lesbian. I could tell by the kindness of our conversation that he was supportive and very fond of his cousin, but I wasn't sure how comfortable he was talking about homosexuality. As we spoke, his tone got heated as we continued, and I certainly didn't feel safe to bring up anything of my own feelings. It wasn't yet the time to talk to him. I would try to have discussions with friends that I thought were safe and trustworthy, but then I'd hear words of disapproval about gays, so I wasn't sure if I should voice my opinions or shy away from speaking. I would drop subtle hints of approval, and quickly quiet down when others' jokes sounded offensive. At the time, I didn't know what to say in defence of the gays. This topic was certainly new to me. I wasn't comfortable either.

I really looked forward to going to my therapy sessions each week. There were no fees, as it was covered under the provincial health plan, so I was very grateful for that. I understood why the television soap opera's would have everyone going to see their therapist. It provided a juicy story line because everyone had issues and secrets, and I was now included. I hated having secrets, and it felt really good to share, because other than with Her, I had no one to talk to who I thought would understand. Each week, I'd sit comfortably in the office lounge chair, and start with, "In the big picture of my life, everything's good. I'm healthy, and this is the most important thing." Then, the details would reveal that I was very unhappy, and feeling a change taking place where, although my marriage was good *in the big picture*, I struggled with my inauthentic relationship with my husband. I always wanted to be with Her, and I had a very difficult time being loving to Him.

For the first time in my life, I was not so good. I felt horrible, and had no answers on how to feel better. I wanted "Her," but I couldn't imagine divorce. I didn't want to hurt "Him." So, now what?

Parallel Lives

We were living parallel lives. Each day, my husband and I would each go to work, take care of the house, take turns with the kids, and then do our own things. We wouldn't argue or fight, but I felt like we were so disconnected, that it was equally disturbing and difficult, and I felt sick. This persisted for a long time. On the weekends, I'd take my daughters to their music lessons at the Conservatory, and while they were practicing in class, I'd walk around downtown, which was in one of the trendiest shopping spots in the city. I'd envy the people sitting amongst their friends at the outdoor cafés, sharing stories and laughing out loud. I felt so lonely, even though I knew I had no real reason to. As I strolled through the streets, I'd have endless conversations in my head on what to do with my relationship with Him. Inevitably, I'd end up in the bookstore, searching in the self-help section. The covers that always caught my eye would have words, like *Lesbian, Women Loving Women, Lesbians and Gays,* and *Life in the Closet.* Secretly, I'd leaf through the chapters for information and clues on things I could do to feel better. I wondered why there were so many lesbian books, yet I felt I had no one safe to talk to. I was still not ready to tell Him, and I didn't want to go to a support group. At the end of the hour stroll, I'd happily retrieve my kids from music class, and take them for ice cream. Our favourite flavour was toasted marshmallow. I'd totally leave my thoughts behind me, and refocus one hundred per cent of my attention to laughing with my kids.

This seemed so easy for me to do. Once we were home, I would be doing my own thing again, and He would be doing his.

My thoughts went from one extreme to another. During family times, I would be devoted to doing family activities, and would concentrate solely on my family. During my quiet times in the car,

I would listen to music. I was intrigued by the words in Melissa Etheridge's songs. They were specific to her unstoppable love for women, and her wanting to be with women. Some even told stories on *coming out,* or stopping the secrets. I would listen to all of them, over and over again. At home, I would sit alone in the den, and search for gay content on TV. I noticed that the shows on TV had started to include gays, and I was so curious, and wanted to see all of the shows. When Ellen DeGeneres *came out* on the Oprah Winfrey Show, I was surprised, thrilled, and really captivated. I looked through all of the stations to watch or listen to her show. Then, I got totally hooked on watching Will and Grace.

I was becoming reassured that maybe being gay was not so unique, or something to hide. Then, by accident (or meant to be), I found the Toronto-filmed show, *Queer as Folk,* a drama television series about the lives and loves of gay friends. Oh, my, how I loved watching it, and I would arrange my schedule so that I could. I'll never forget the day when I was watching *Queer as Folk* on TV, and my daughter Nicole walked into the den. Feeling guilty and secretive, I quickly changed the channel. Nicole asked me what I was watching, and I replied, "Nothing, really, just flipping through shows." She then said, "Oh, I know that show you were watching; it's *Queer as Folk.*" Well, my face felt flushed, and I couldn't believe that she knew the theme song from the show. She went on to say that her friend from school acted in the show. She played one of the high school kids. My daughters had all gone to a dramatic arts school, and they were more in tune with the gay world than I was.

Well, it took my own kids to keep me current on what is going on in the world. My daughter was more in touch with the shows with gay content than I was.

How long could I keep my secret quiet? How long did I want to keep a secret?

Hiding Behind Busy

My life was really busy, just like everyone else's. But the term *multitasking* was an understatement, even in the quietest of times. The clinic had gone through two expansion renovations to accommodate the increase in innovative programs and client population numbers. Business was really good, and I continued to work long hours to maximize its growth. I needed to travel a lot to our new satellite clinics around the city, as well as put in the hours to treat the patients, and complete office work. There were times that I'd stay working on a proposal deadline at the clinic, right through the night, and return home in the morning, just in time to make breakfast and drive my three kids to school. Sometimes I'd go right back to work, and when I was dead tired, I'd go home for a quick, rejuvenation nap.

At the end of my regular work days, I'd pick up my kids from school and take them to their after-school tutoring lessons, doctor's appointments, and sporting activities, or to a friend's home to socialize. In between, I'd find time to shop for groceries or finish other errands for home or the clinic. After I picked them up to bring them home, I'd make dinner, feed the family, and then finish up the evening doing the laundry, tidying the house, preparing the following days school lunches, and, lastly, finishing my notes and to-do list for the clinic the next day.

On my days off, I enjoyed meeting girlfriends for lunch. We'd share stories just about everything. Sometimes I'd try to drop subtle hints about my time spent with Her, or hope that the topic of gays came up so that I could get a sense of how they felt about gays. I'd get so close to telling them how I was feeling about Her, and my difficulties in keeping close to Him, but I couldn't. If I told anyone my feelings about Her, then I'd have to tell them to keep the secret. If I did that, I was bringing them into my life of deception. Otherwise, I'd risk that He would find out before I was ready for him to know. I wasn't ready to take the risk of hurting or angering Him, or, even worse, breaking up our marriage.

So, my life with Her was safely and quietly protected within me. I'd somehow find time, in between running from one place to another, to see Her. Connecting on the Internet was new in our lives, and very exciting because I was able to connect to Her often, without anyone else knowing. There always seemed to be openings during the day on the weekends for us to be connected in one way or another. She was building a new family home with her husband, and needed to choose the cabinets, colours, appliances, and furniture. I was very willing to help with that, just so I could be with Her. I'd meet Her at stores, and go to her home as it was being built. None of this was a secret because my husband and friends knew that she was building a new home, and knew that I was joining her when she was shopping.

What they didn't know was that we couldn't wait to hold hands when we were driving in the car together, or kiss and hug when we found a private space. They didn't see the looks of love we shared, or hear the love songs that we sang together. These were the special moments that I cherished and wanted in my life, all day long. As the days passed, She and I managed to be together often, but the goodbyes seemed to become more upsetting and difficult. Often, when I drove away from her house, I'd have intense cramping, and piercing pain in my belly. Constipation would follow, and I'd feel miserable going about my day. Over the counter medications weren't helping, and I was sure this had nothing to do with M.S. I decided to just ignore the pain, and maybe it would go away.

Stabbing Belly Pain

Oddly enough, I was happy that She and her husband were building this beautiful custom home, with all of the latest designs. (I chose to be happy, despite the sharp stomach pains I often had during the day.) But I never connected the fact that she was building a new home with her husband; and therefore, it meant that she'd never be building a life with me (The stabbing pains were getting worse.), even though, when we talked about our dreams, we'd both say that we wanted to move far away together, and live in paradise. Maybe I knew deep down that these dreams were just talk, and my life would never really change. (Ouch; the pains were piercing, causing me to buckle forward until they slowly subsided, or would they?)

When I found time to go for my therapy sessions, to talk about my life with Him and Her, I felt so much better, knowing that I was sorting through options on how I could work through my life of hiding. (I didn't have intense stomach pain during my therapy sessions.) I needed to work on being honest, and feeling more peaceful. At first, my therapist asked me straight out if I wanted to divorce my husband, and I would quickly answer *no*. Then, my therapist would ask me how I would feel if we were to divorce, and my friends stopped being my friends. Well, I would reply that that would never happen because we had been friends for years, and that didn't seem possible.

At each session, my therapist asked me the same questions, and my replies didn't change. She said, in many cases, the friends that you thought were friends would choose sides, and she made it known that I would probably lose my friends. I didn't believe her, or didn't want to believe her. (Okay, sometimes I had pain during therapy.) I was quite confident that I really didn't think I'd ever lose my friends. She certainly got me wondering, though, about my relationships with my husband and my friends. She again suggested that I attend the support group for lesbians. I still wasn't ready to confront my fears, and go to the group.

Instead, I was often thinking about more ways to find occasions to be with Her. I got busier helping Her with the building, packing, and the moving preparations. (The belly pains were more frequent and intense.) Since I was an expert packer when it came to moving, I offered to help her pack up the items in her existing house. I would go to Her house often, and pack up each room, like kitchenware, or books or trinkets from the shelves in the den. We'd be together for hours: packing, dancing in the kitchen, then packing, singing out loud to our favourite songs, then packing, and cooking and laughing till we were crying from just being happy together. We couldn't get enough of being with each other, until we'd crash in one another's arms, and then blissfully fall asleep.

I'd wake up just a few hours later, and know that I'd have to drive home. During my drive home, I'd say to myself, "My life is stupid, and I don't like it anymore, but I don't know what to do." I still knew that I was getting closer to telling Him, but I was so scared because I didn't want to hurt him or my family. This is all that I'd think about. I didn't want to disappoint my friends, and I wasn't ready to change my life, but my busy days of hiding were causing me too much worry and nervous tension. I was feeling deceitful, and I no longer wanted to feel that way. For too long, I seemed to be wavering back and forth between wanting Her and a new life, to not wanting my life to change at all.

Destiny directs us to go places where we must go, when we won't go to the places on our own.

To the O.R. STAT!

I was feeling so stressed, and frequently suffered from sharp, stabbing belly pains. The pain was too severe to ignore. I still continued to go to work, and took care of my family, but with the unrelenting, agonizing, piercing pains, I ended up going for medical testing that seemed to go on forever. The preliminary medical tests revealed nothing. Then, following a day of more testing in the hospital, I was told I could be Lactose intolerant, so I was advised to go off dairy, which I did. After several months of being on the dairy-free diet, the pains got even worse. I was then diagnosed with irritable bowel disease. I was given yet another special diet, and I followed it for 3 more months. The pain persisted. I had more tests where liquids were pumped into my bowels, and I was tipped upside down. I had no definitive diagnosis, and the cramping was excruciating. I went to work with stomach pain, while continuing to drive my kids around, and spend time helping Her pack.

Unfortunately, I continued to feel awful about my secretive life but didn't know how to change it.

The finishing touches on Her new home were complete, and the moving date was planned for Saturday, October 12, 2001. I told Her that I'd be at her home on Saturday, and looked forward to helping out with the move. On the Friday prior to the moving day, I had very sharp pains, and felt weak and ill, but I went to work and stayed until the end of the day. I then picked up my kids from school, and took them home. After giving them a snack, I told them that I was going to go to the hospital because I wasn't feeling very well, and wanted to get some medication for my stomach ache. I assured them that I'd be back before supper.

Friday, October 11, 2001
4:00pm – Drive myself to North York General Hospital, and park at Emergency.
4:15pm – Assessment at ER triage: c/o distended abdomen and severe pain.
4:30pm – Asked to wait in waiting room.
5:00pm – I keel over and vomit blood in the waiting room, and call for help. I'm immediately put on a stretcher and taken for examination.
My husband is notified and arrives quickly.
Detailed testing, excruciating pain, bloated belly.
Elevated heart rate, sweating, dangerously low blood pressure.
In and out of consciousness.
My husband gets my approval, and signs waivers to authorize abdominal surgery.
I remember a vague explanation that there was a small chance that the surgery may result in the need for a colostomy, where I would have an external bag at the side of my abdomen to collect feces. I feel the IV placed in my arm, and an oxygen mask on my nose and mouth...I'm out like a light.
11:00pm – surgery is successful: hemicolectomy to repair a cecal volvulus.

Recovery room: My eyes open; I smile when I see my husband. I instantly gently stroke the sides of my abdomen with my hands. I don't feel a faecal bag. I ask the nurse if I've had a colostomy, and the nurse's reply is *no*. I'm told that the surgeon was very pleased with the results, and he expected a full recovery.

I thank God for my second chance, close my teary eyes, quiet my tranquil mind, and slip into a deep and peaceful sleep.

Saturday, October 12, 2001 – I woke up in the hospital bed with a nasogastric tube in my nose, suction tube in my side, a urinary catheter, IVs, and a big bandage on my belly, with 15 staples holding me together. I wouldn't be eating solids for 6–10 days.

Epiphany

My 101-year-old uncle used to say, with gratitude, "I woke up!" whenever I would call him on the telephone to ask him, "How are you today, uncle?" On the first morning following my surgery, I was grateful to know that I woke up. I had just had half of my large intestine removed. While I was open on the operating table, I had my appendix taken out as well. On high doses of morphine, and feeling very little pain, I knew that everything was going to be OK. I looked around my room, and noticed ten, or maybe even more than fifteen, bouquets of brilliantly coloured flowers on the windowsill and tabletops. Get well cards were stacked up, just waiting for me to open. I felt so honoured and privileged to have received so many kind gestures encouraging me to get better. That first day, I had an influx of visitors who were so surprised that I ended up in the hospital having life saving emergency surgery. I remember feeling all teary when my husband arrived with my 3 adorable daughters. Tears trickled down my cheeks. Me, being in the hospital, with tubes up my nose and an IV in my arm, and a big bandage on my belly, was an alarming surprise to everyone. I had hoped that my family would have felt relief when they saw that I was smiling and joking, and telling them that I planned on being home real soon.

My husband's family and my friends also came by on the very first day. One of my (then) close girlfriends asked if She had been told, and when I said *no*, she assured me that she would call her for me. My friend had obviously known that She was important to me. I was panicked when I remembered that I was supposed to be helping Her move into her new home, but I wasn't there helping. I was, instead, being attended to by doctors, nurses, and physiotherapists, who insisted that I get up and walk. What was She thinking? I sadly reflected on what had just happened—why now? Another message that my secrets were causing my health to breakdown? [I just recently learned that Coming Out Day is October 11. Coincidence?]

On the Sunday, I had visitors coming and going throughout the day. He had brought my three daughters, and we spoke about their regular daily activities. I don't remember sadness in the room; we all celebrated that the surgery was a success, and that I'd be home in about a week. My in-laws, and so many close friends, dropped in, interested in the stories of the events leading up to the surgery. Many of the people that I worked with came with their families to wish me well. My room was always filled with visitors throughout the day, and I was busy answering phone calls up until the early evening. When I had first learned that I had the surgery in order to save my life, I needed to make light of it. I joked with my friends, saying now that I've had half my colon removed, I'm no longer full of shit. It was certainly true from an anatomical perspective, but in reality, it was now time I took it one step further to truly clean up my life and my irreplaceable health.

Then, at the end of the evening, She arrived. I almost drowned in my own tears, feeling so happy, and at the same time, feeling a fear and urgency in wanting my life to be different. She stayed right next to me for a long time that night. I rested in the bed, just happy to be alive and close to her.

It was after She left, when the room was quiet, that millions of thoughts went through my mind. I scanned the room, counting the many bouquets of flowers brought and sent with prayers of wellness. I pictured the faces around my bed, smiling and laughing in hopes that I'd feel better soon. I cherished the warm love and support from my husband and daughters as they kissed me hello when they entered to greet me. And I couldn't forget "Her" visit that prompted me to realize that it was time for me to become authentic with my family, my friends, and finally, myself.

Chapter 6

Authentic Life

Personal Growth

It was when my friend, Jan, said to me, one evening soon after my surgery, "Everything went really well with your surgery, didn't it?" and I gratefully said, "Yes." Jan smiled, and then said to me, "Your physio practice is growing, isn't it? And your kids are all healthy and doing well in school, aren't they? And your husband is fine, and you are really happy, aren't you?" My confident reply, again, was, "Yes, yes, and yes." Jan then went on to ask, "Do you want everything to be even better?" I looked at the intensity in Jan's eyes, and felt the enthusiasm in the energy surrounding her, and said, "Yes," while holding back my excitement, and wondering what more she had to say. She then went on to tell me about The Landmark Forum, a personal development course that she'd just completed, and she thought that I'd really enjoy it, and would definitely benefit from taking it. In less than a week, I researched it online, and then I enrolled in the open forum, which was a trial that offered a chance at me becoming more authentic in my life. I really connected with the introduction, and soon after, I signed up to attend, in the hopes that I would better understand myself, and improve my own in-authenticities. I so needed to learn how to clear my conscience that had become tainted from my secret love for Her.

More and more desperate to change, I attended The Landmark Forum, with an open mind and willingness to risk exposing my vulnerabilities for all to see. Attending the four-day course, with over 125 strangers that I'd probably never see again, allowed me to feel somewhat safe. But I was taught that society and my Armenian church, and not to mention every other religious institution, made it very clear that a woman in love with another woman was wrong, and it was an abomination. Afraid of judgment, I initially resisted sharing when asked to tell my story. Instead, I listened to others, story after story, after story: sons and daughters weren't speaking to their parents, or vice versa; husbands and wives were keeping secrets from one another; staff were deceiving their bosses; and family clans hadn't spoken with each other for years. Not only were the stories filled with secrets, misunderstandings, judgement, and poor communication, but it also seemed that many ended in health struggles, sickness, and disease. So familiar and accepting of my own scenario, mine seemed less complicated, less angry, and certainly not criminal, as many of the stories were. I wondered what the group reaction would be if I disclosed my years of living a double life.

When we broke out into small groups, I slowly shared fragments of my story to observe the responses. My group's remarks were surprisingly so accepting, supportive, and kind. The continued conversations were validating and reassuring. Following the second day, I understood that I owed it to my husband, children, and friends, and, of course, to myself, to speak out and tell the truth. I mostly sat silent but still felt an overwhelming relief that I had shared even just a bit. I knew it was time to open up completely. I felt less shame, and more confident than I had felt in a very long time. I was ready to speak. In just 2 days, I learned that by keeping truths hidden, and not having honest conversations with the people in my life that mattered most, I was limiting my self-expression and optimal success and happiness. My homework on the second night was to have a loving conversation with my husband, whom I had been inauthentic, and express my truths. I was then requested to return to the course the third day, and share with the group my experiences.

I had loved "Her" for over 20 years. Finally, I listened, and even understood that I had been living in a closet with the doors closed tight. I was ready to open the doors, speak my truths, and admit this to "Him."

"I'm Coming Out"

My homework was clear, and I intended to do it. I had taken this personal development course in order to put myself on a path to authenticity. I no longer wanted deception; I didn't want to pretend, and I didn't want secrets anymore. My body had been whispering danger signals to me for too many years, but I hadn't been listening. First, it was the signs and symptoms of Multiple Sclerosis. When I changed my path, the symptoms diminished, and I felt stronger and healthier. I felt so well physically and emotionally that my urgent, desperate love for Her resurfaced, and She was back in my life.

Again, on the path of deceit, my health failed once more, landing me in the hospital's operating room. How many times did I have to fall ill to realize that my secrets, and the stress they caused, were the big contributors to my failing health? This time, I understood that I had two choices on how to proceed. One, I could continue my not so perfect family life, and painfully deny my being a lesbian, and suffer forever, or, two, tell Him the truth, and decide with him how to go forward respectfully, in a way that would make sense and be fair for all of us. I knew that for many years I had stopped seeing Her, and tried to reject her, and ignore my feelings for her. I can't explain why, but by stopping my relationship with Her, I was denying a core part of who I was, and it just didn't work. The best explanation I can say now is, "Life, love, and heterosexuality, and homosexuality, isn't very complicated, and, in fact, we are all very much alike, since we all want to love and be loved."

I had been sincere in all parts of my life, except when it came to my love for Her. My feelings of being ashamed and wrong, while going along with society's teachings, took over my life, and kept me from being whom I was meant to be. For all those years, I felt that my motives were honourable. I was constantly in the mode of survival. I finally realized, to maintain my integrity, I had to tell the truth, and clear my conscience. After years of on and off physical and emotional health challenges, I was willing to risk upsetting my husband, family, friends, and my entire social network, and even Her, so that I could be completely honest and sincere for myself.

Having gained the confidence and validation from my small group, I was ready.

At midnight that evening, I was determined to have a heart to heart talk with my husband. Sitting close together on the couch while holding his hands, I looked in his eyes, and I shared it all. At first, I mentioned to Him that I wanted to talk about some of our recent conversations that had troubled me, especially while they turned to arguments. I apologized by saying that I was so, so sorry that I hadn't told him the truth in answer to his many questions about how I was feeling, and if I was hiding something. Following back and forth discussions, I then told him straight out that I had been in love with Her for a long time.

I remember that He went from being shocked to surprised, to, not being so surprised. In fact, I suspected that although he really hadn't known about our intimate loving relationship, he knew we had been much more than best friends for years, and he had started to suspect that something was different between us, and that I was hiding something. I repeated that I had never wanted to hurt him. I hadn't wanted to break up our family, and I wasn't considering divorce. I wasn't sure how we could go forward, but we'd talk about it and figure it out. As we continued talking through the night, I noticed that He wasn't angry but sad. His voice didn't get loud and tough, but he collapsed into being quiet and fatigued. I knew that night, that my life with Him could never be the same. With tearful eyes, we hugged and fell asleep.

*I was so worried, so sad, and yet so relieved—oh, so relieved—
no more secrets.*

Authenticity

My need for authenticity drove me to have the conversation
that would change small parts of my life that very next day. I no
longer had secrets from my husband. The secrets had been
tormenting me for years, and suddenly I felt free. The next morning
following the conversation that I feared, I returned to my class at
The Landmark Forum, and although I didn't know what life had in
store for me, the stress and guilt that I'd lived with for so long was
gone. When the facilitator of the class asked for volunteers to step
forward and share with the rest of the class their experiences from
the night before, I hesitated, still stunned from what I had said.
Instead, I sat and listened. One gentleman got up and told his story
about his long distance telephone conversation with his father, in
Italy. He hadn't spoken to his father in over 10 years because of a
past argument, and he didn't even remember what it was about.
They spoke for an hour, and he made a promise to his father that
he'd visit him soon. The audience stood and cheered for a long
time. Then, a woman, smiling from ear to ear, shared that she had
called her boss, and asked him for a raise. She'd wanted to do that
for over a year but couldn't. She went on to say that her boss
assured her that he'd give her a raise, and that she should speak to
him at the office first thing Monday morning. Again, there was a
loud cheer as the audience stood in celebration. Another young
man stood up to say that he told his mother that he was gay. He
said that his mother said that she had suspected all along and was
so happy that he finally told her.

One person after another stood up and shared the details of
conversations that hadn't happened for years but that should have.
The conversations were referred to as breakthroughs that changed
people's lives. At the end of each story, the audience would shout
out in support of each person for what they had achieved, following

just two days of encouragement and permission to follow their heart and have the meaningful conversation that they had been wanting to have for a long time. I then felt it was my turn, so I stood up, and nervously but joyfully walked towards the stage. I looked at the 125 people looking back at me. I told the audience that I was about to say something that I hadn't shared with anyone in 20 years. I took a deep breath, and slowly said that I sat with my husband of 20 years last night, and told him that I was in love with a woman, and had been for years. I then said out loud, for the first time, to the audience and to myself, that *I was gay*. The audience applauded and cheered in support, but I think that I was the one most surprised and amazed. This conversation was so new to me. I was really uncomfortable using the label *lesbian*, and a bit more comfortable with the term *gay*. I had to get to understand, and get used to, this conversation, as much as everyone else did.

Following the storytelling breakthrough celebrations, we broke out into small groups to review what we had just learned from each other. It was apparent that many people aren't very good at having real conversations. So many people aren't skilled at listening or speaking, or understanding how to achieve the many possibilities open to them. I witnessed that participating in a conversation that's revealing and truthful becomes transformational for all those involved. Everyone in the room seemed to rest comfortably in a place of pure relief for themselves and those around them.

I was feeling empowered and courageous at first, having been encouraged by the positive energy of the group, and by having had the important conversations. Then I stopped and wondered, what had I done? And what was I to do now?

No Big Changes, Not Right Away

My secret was out to the most important person in my life: my husband. I felt a new sense of calm, and my thoughts were free to think in a relaxed and uncluttered way. I had loving, detailed, connected conversations with Him at the very beginning by revealing more information, and at the same time, understanding that while I was in a state of emotional relief, with no plans to make immediate changes, I was sure that He felt confused, unhappy, and awkwardly unsettled. I had lived on and off for 20 years, thinking and feeling awkward in my own skin, and I wasn't even sure how my life had reached that point. How did I expect Him to begin to understand the complexities of how I had managed to hide my feelings? I also knew that just because my new information was shared, I needed to remind myself, and him, that big changes didn't need to happen, not immediately anyways, not until we thought things through, and not until we understood the options on how to move forward.

I was finally admitting to myself that I'd been terribly unfair to Him, and my family. I was feeling that I needed to take things slow, and be open to his questions and comments and concerns. I'd always been upfront and dedicated with regard to my care and love for Him and our family life. I'd just made more time than I should have for Her in my life. But I just didn't' know how else to live. I repeated to Him how sorry I was, while knowing that the words I'm sorry could never excuse my deception, nor repair the pain that he felt. When I shared with Her that I told my husband and some of my friends that I was in love with her, she was deeply upset with me. She stated that I had betrayed the trust she had in me for keeping our little secret. I understood her point, for she had no intention of telling her husband, nor any of her friends or family. Well, now I felt really troubled, because now He was unhappy, and She was unhappy, and I was in the middle, feeling really confused because I felt delightfully relieved and liberated. Telling Him was the best thing I could have done to begin the process of repairing and moving forward for a real and authentic relationship.

I worked hard to reconnect, and He and I got along really well, as the truths were told and the tensions dissipated. We went on dates together, and we became friends again. We joined in on the many family gatherings, and went on vacations with the kids. Everything seemed to be good. I was happy when at work, pleased to drive my kids to their school and after school programs, and continued my therapy sessions regularly. We had talked about separating, but I was really thrown off guard when, one day, He said to me that he'd spoken to his lawyer, who suggested that we should have an official separation date. Wow, things were changing faster and sooner than I expected. And it was the right thing to do, so we chose an official separation date.

When I had discussions with Her, she seemed to be less angry, but I continued to feel some tension. We both cherished the romantic dreams, but I was more serious about wanting and making real permanent changes. Knowing that I was making different life changes, she would often say to me, "Don't leave Him for me, but leave Him because you want a brand new life for yourself." Well, yikes, I wasn't really ready to leave Him and change my family yet. I thought I was leaving Him for Her, but I guess I shouldn't have. I first wanted to be sure of my feelings, and more confident that I preferred the relationship and intimacy of being with a woman instead of a man. It didn't take long until I was sure, realizing that I had been living this life of loving Her for 20 years. I was finished being married to a man. I knew I was a lesbian.

I confessed to my therapist during an emotional session that, although I was happy in the big picture of my life, I was still concealing a pivotal part of me that wanted to get out. I had become authentic with my husband, and had formally separated, but this just wasn't enough. What about my authenticity with my family and friends?

New Directions

When I left my therapist's office, she gave me the updated, current flyer from New Directions, a community program that offered information and assistance for women. The calendar was full of events on a variety of topics. Circled in red was an evening support group workshop, *Married Women with Questions About Their Sexuality.* This time, I was curious, and open to going to the support group to meet other women who may have had the same questions and concerns that I had.

Conscious of my sweaty palms and rapid heartbeat, I nervously but excitedly entered through the doorway of the building, where the sign read, New Directions. I certainly felt like I was in the right place. After checking in at reception, I entered the bare meeting room, and sat beside the facilitator. There must have been 20 empty folding chairs positioned in a large circle around the room. One by one, women quietly entered the room and sat down. Proudly, I sat. I had finally conjured up the courage to go to a meeting on my own, for married women questioning their sexuality, and I smiled secretly. I was so surprised when the 20 chairs were filled, and I was relieved that I didn't feel out of place. Many of the women were in the same age range as me, and they looked like they could've been any one of my friends. I felt at ease. The facilitator opened up the conversation with a short bio about herself. She then asked the group members to do the same, one by one. When no one offered to start, I volunteered to go first.

"Hello, my name is Audrey Kouyoumdjian. I'm 45 years old, and have been happily married to my husband for 21 years. We have 3 wonderful daughters, between the ages of 8 and 17. I work as a physiotherapist. I've also been in an intimate loving relationship with my best girlfriend for even more than 21 years. She knows I'm at this meeting but preferred not to attend because she said that she didn't need support or therapy. I feel I do. I married my husband for all of the right reasons: love, admiration, respect, same cultural background, and similar goals. He'd be a good father to my children, and I wanted to get married and live happily ever after. I'm now troubled because I'm in love with my girlfriend, and would like to have her in my life honestly. I've told my husband, and I'm trying to understand and sort out what I should do next."

One by one, the women shared their stories. I felt like this storytelling was becoming a familiar and satisfying emotional release. Many of the women were married to men, many had children, many had female lovers, and many had the same questions wondering what to do next. Then, the last woman spoke up, and started by pointing to me, and said, "Whatever she said, Ditto." She then went on to say that she had known for more than 5 years that she was a lesbian, and had an open and honest relationship with her husband of 25 years. Wow, I was impressed and encouraged to know that she and her husband were making their relationship and family life work out in their own way. I wondered if I could do the same. I didn't want to divorce my husband, or change our family life, but I didn't really understand how I'd be happier not changing, or what other options I could consider, or what they would look like. When all of the women had shared their stories, it was clear that I wasn't alone or unique. It was clear that I could learn from the experiences of other women like me. It was clear that I didn't need to make big changes right away, or at all. But what was most clear was that there was no right or wrong way to live through this, but that it would take loving communication, understanding, and a lot of education, because I certainly had no previous experience.

I was about to go on the journey: From Straight Wife to Lesbian Life

Fresh Start, New Approach

When the meeting had finished, Carol walked toward me and introduced herself. She was the woman who had pointed to me, and said, "Ditto to what she said," when it came her turn to share. We laughed at the fact that we had lead somewhat similar lives, having been married for over 20 years; we each had 3 kids, we both enjoyed physical fitness, were in the health care field, and we were both interested in understanding our growing need and feelings for women. I was relieved to know I wasn't alone in my experience, and I had someone that I could talk to and share the thoughts and feelings that had been supressed for a long time. Our conversation in just the first few minutes was rapid fire, with similar and sometimes-identical experiences, and lots of excitement—so much so that we decided to go and continue the discussion at the nearby coffee shop. Carol had driven to the meeting with a friend, so the three of us sat drinking coffee while chatting for hours. I remember driving home that night and feeling so refreshed that I had met women like me, and I had a new friend. I could finally be open and feel safe when being myself. To my delightful surprise, just fifteen minutes later when I arrived home that night, I opened my computer, and I noticed an email from Carol that read, "Nice to meet you Audrey...." It was so nice to feel connected at a time where I often felt so alone.

My day-to-day activities didn't change much, but I was so much happier having gone to the support group workshop and meeting like-minded women. I really wanted to start telling people how I felt, but I knew that I couldn't. Not yet. I felt more content that He knew, but I was feeling restless and concerned when thinking that my feelings about keeping quiet were changing. I was ready, and now wanted to tell my sisters the news. I wanted them to know that I was a lesbian. I knew that once I told my sisters, I'd be starting an entire confession session. He insisted that I not tell anyone, and to keep it to ourselves. He wanted me to continue life as we had been. I could continue to see Her, but not tell anyone. This sounded like the same scenario that She wanted. On the one hand, the thought of not changing our family life was very comforting. But on the other hand, I couldn't see how I could continue this false façade. I'd still be hiding.

I was sad for Him. He wanted our life to go on together. But I didn't feel that I was the ideal wife for him any longer. It wasn't fair for him, and I couldn't continue seeing Him sad. I felt that this secret needed to be out, and especially with my sisters. If I told my sisters, I'd see and understand how they would feel when they heard the news. I went over the conversation in my head so many times, and was convinced being authentic was the right thing to do, and this was the right time. Once in a while, my sisters and I would meet in New York City for a reunion. I decided to organize a birthday reunion for one of my sisters. This birthday smoke screen reduced my anxiety in explaining why we were getting together, even though I had a full agenda and a lot to share. He and I had some conflict as the trip neared, but I told him how important it was to me, and I repeated that I didn't want to keep secrets anymore. I tried to understand his position. I also thought that the longer we kept this secret going, the more difficult our relationship would become. I knew that this was all so new, and next to impossible for Him to really understand, but I thought that I needed to tell my sisters, and they would want to know.

I felt convinced, and booked my flight to N.Y.C. to feel the joy in being authentic.

Chapter 7

My Secret is Out: Ending Gossip

Full Confessions

Rather than coming out to both of my sisters at the same time, I decided to tell just one, and see her response. I thought that my discussing the news with just one would reduce my feelings of awkwardness, and probably hers too. So, one evening, I first sat alone with Chris, and I tried to present the story as simple and calm as possible. I spoke a little, and then paused to wait for her reaction. She was very surprised at first, but as we spoke about the situations through the past many years, she understood, and saw my story unfold and make sense. Some parts of my relationship with Her were for the first time explainable and understandable to my sister. Other parts of my life demonstrated that it was not at all a surprise that I was a lesbian, and that I had been in love with Her for many years.

When I saw that nothing bad happened, and Chris wasn't angry, upset, or bothered in any way, I asked her if she would be able to support me while I told Wendy. She said she'd be very supportive, and assured me that although Wendy may not receive the news as well, that given some time, she would be caring and kind because she loved me. Well, we talked all night, and as the two of them went back and forth taking turns asking questions and telling stories about their gay friends, they were curious to know all about my feeling on when I knew, and how I knew, and why I was telling them now. They wondered if I'd get divorced, and asked a lot of questions about my current relationship with my husband. I told them that I didn't plan on making big changes right away, but I had no idea what would happen through time. I said that I never wanted to hurt anyone, and the reason that my privacy had lasted so long was because I felt that I was protecting my family.

I had always had my daughters and husband's feelings on my mind. I wanted to keep joy in our lives, and changing our family life would challenge the happiness that we had. I also thought I was protecting myself from feeling embarrassed, disrespected, and rejected. I further explained that I thought my M.S. and colon health issues were connected to my secrets, and to my unhappiness, when I couldn't be with Her. I now had to *come out* to better my health. I went on to explain that it was now time for me to tell my family and friends that I was a lesbian. I told them that I had gone to a support group that my therapist had recommended, and that I had met many women in the same situation as me. My sisters were very surprised that I had found such a workshop, and also so pleased that I had a place where I could speak honestly with women who would understand me.

They over emphasised that it could be tough when I tell my friends because they won't be as understanding and caring as sisters. I agreed that my sisters were my pillars but doubted that my friends wouldn't be supportive. I told them that my therapist had definitely told me many times that most of my friends would have difficulty, and I may lose them. The three of us talked about my *coming out*, on and off, during our three-day visit. At the end of the trip, I assured them that we could talk about this as much as they wished, and they could talk with their friends, and that they could follow up and ask me questions, or share their thoughts as often as they like. I certainly knew that this conversation was new for us all.

Wendy then said to me, "When Ellen DeGeneres came out, it was news, and everyone was announcing that Ellen was gay. Now, it's no longer news, and the discussions are now about what a great person she is." *I want my story to be news, then see the news fade, and hear the discussions about my joyful and healthy life.*

Coffee Breaks the News

I felt like I was walking on thin ice as I wondered how to go forward to break the news to more of my family and friends. My husband was quite firm on never telling his brother, sister-in-law, or mother. I felt awful that I wanted desperately to do something that He was so opposed to, and I was bothered that I was being asked to continue to deceive people. If I could have come out without hurting anyone, I would have. I reminded Him that I remembered when I had first shared with his brother that I had M.S., many years following my diagnosis. My brother-in-law had mentioned to me then that he'd have preferred if I had told him sooner. I had agreed with him, and this time I thought it was best if I were up front with him now. My brother-in-law may have been more understanding in this situation if we'd shared more at that time.

Debating discussions between my husband and I went back and forth for many weeks. My anger was building from our conflict, so I tried to remain calm. I told Him that I'd be telling his brother and sister-in-law, but I agreed not to tell his eighty-year-old mother, since she probably wouldn't understand, and the unknown may cause her unnecessary worry. I told Him how sorry I was, and that I knew that neither of us could be satisfied, because he wanted to keep the secrets, and I wanted to be free of secrets. It was difficult for me to move forward, but I had to start; otherwise, my awkward, nauseating feelings of deceit that I had lived with would continue. I told Him that I just had to tell his brother. I tried to explain that I still felt safe since our life wouldn't need to change just because his brother knew I was a lesbian. I'm sure, in the end, He wasn't pleased. I was too excited to finally speak out, and admittedly, I was not sensitive to His feelings. I didn't want to hold back. I felt that I had held back for far too long.

Each time I opened up to tell the people close to me that I was gay, I felt an unbelievable relief, and was surprised to see that the conversations were positive. When my immediate family knew, I wanted my friends to know. I arranged gatherings at coffee shops with five to ten friends to share my news. It went something like this: "I have something to share." With the first group of friends, they all gasped, and seemed to ready themselves for the worst news. After I had said that I was gay, and had been for a long time, many replied that they thought I was going to tell them that I had cancer, was going to die, or that I had some other tragic news. Many said they were relieved when at the end all I said was that I was gay. I went out for coffee with different groups of friends of mine for a month. Each night, while driving home, I couldn't believe how relieved I felt. I was reassured that I was doing the right thing. I had to be mindful of other's feelings, but I had to continue my journey of living as I was meant to live.

Every time that I felt good at the end of the conversations, I wanted to open up to more people. When I had, in my eyes, successfully come out to my Armenian friends, I knew it was time to tell the people who worked with me, and that included my business partner of more than 15 years. I hesitated telling my business partner, not because I didn't think she would support me as her friend and colleague, but because I had the feeling she wouldn't want to listen or try to understand, because of her strong Christian teachings.

Immediately upon "coming out," nothing seemed different. But very soon after, to my surprise, I faced unexpected, deliberate exclusion. Did my friends intend to hurt me on purpose? I was surprised to see but very determined to look past all of the hurtful and adverse reactions from people I considered my friends.

Being Christian?

Since I felt so good during my first *coming out* conversations, I didn't stop to wonder what underlying less positive thoughts people could be thinking. But that's because I didn't want to even think that there could be any negative feelings. My business partner's strict Christian beliefs certainly did concern me. I had read the gay hate signs, and heard about the teen killings and gay suicides, while all in the name of religion. My business partner, with my approval, had hired her pastor's wife to be our clinic's secretary. I was respectful of my environment with strict Christian staff, and needed to understand how to have a conversation about being gay, and be on the same side as the church. I knew that my God loved me. What better way to get some suggestions on how to have a successful *coming out* conversation with my Christian business partner than to have a meeting with her Pastor?

So, I met with him to ask for his opinion on how I should prepare myself for my conversations. During a couple of enjoyable hours, while sipping coffee and sharing my most intimate thoughts and stories, I was able to cover the four points that I thought were most important to me. 1) I had been in love with my girlfriend for years before, and during, my marriage with my husband. 2) I had suffered repeated physical and emotional health challenges during those years because my heart and spirit were fractured. 3) I had decided, with the coaching of my therapist, self help books, and personal development courses, that I needed to be authentic to improve my health and the relationships with my husband, my family, and friends. 4) I needed to tell my business partner so that she would know a core part of me that had been hidden for years because of my fears regarding the loss of my social connections. As I waited with interest to hear her Pastor's words of wisdom, I understood from his soft smile that his comments were going to be kind. His elaborated lessons confirmed that he would convey an explanation that would protect his church's teachings, and my business relationship. He repeated that Christians would always love. He thought that my business partner would always be kind, even when she wouldn't like hearing, and might be quite upset, that I was gay. He wasn't quite sure if she would support me or not. I wasn't sure either at that point, but I was doing my best to pave the way towards a conversation between the two of us, that would end as positive as possible. What I really wanted was for her to listen and honestly hear me. I hoped that she would ask me questions to learn things that she might not understand. I hoped she would know that I was born this way, and that I was doing all I could to open up and have loving conversations with my family, my staff, and my friends

While my business partner and I were both at the clinic one day, I mentioned to her that I had something I wanted to say, and asked if we could speak privately in the office that we shared. I remember well that the conversation was short. While I was sitting at my desk and she was standing at hers, I said that I had something important to say, which I had been waiting to tell her for a long time. I smiled and stated that this was no longer private or a secret; it was for everyone to hear. I took a big breath and told her that I was gay. The shock on her face told me that she didn't know what to say, but then she blurted out, "Oh, my gosh, I don't even know you!" I rebutted, "Sure you do, I'm made up of over 100 parts, and you have known 99 parts for years. I slowed down, smiled, and said, "I introduced you to your husband, and I was your maid of honour at your wedding; I am the Godmother to your eldest son. I've been your connected business partner for over 15 years; I'm a physiotherapist, a mom, and a sister, and I am your dear friend, and a Christian. You just didn't know that I loved a woman." She then said, "But how will your kids turn out?" and I could only think to myself, and then blurted out "I don't know... How will your kids turn out?" She left the office, and left the clinic; the next day, I found out that she left the country for a getaway retreat, to be with her friend so she could put the pieces together.

The Shotgun Clause

I didn't expect my business partner, of many years, to react to my news by immediately leaving for a week, and going to visit her friend in the USA. She didn't tell me that she was leaving, or why, but I had heard from my staff that she had to leave to console herself, with a friend, regarding our conversation. At that point, I thought that we both needed consoling. If my business partner were so distraught, I would have wanted her to express her feelings in more ways than when she had asked "Why didn't you tell me sooner?" I had said, "Because I was afraid of this!" I would have welcomed comments, like, "I am upset because I don't understand. This must have been hard for you to keep secrets for all of these years. Please explain what it means to you, being gay. Will being gay change our relationship? Will being gay change the way we work together?" I really didn't understand why this was affecting her so badly but hoped it would be clearer when she returned from her getaway trip.

We never did have a compassionate conversation about me being gay. We never did communicate together to ease the tension that we both felt. We each went to work every day, and attended to our specific jobs, but the joy of working together was gone. Each day, I felt tension and resentment. Our friendship was deteriorating, and our conversations were business only. A year passed, and my being gay was the elephant in the room. When her mother-in-law, whom I had know for 20 years, came to the office for a visit, she would barely say hello to me, when in the past, we would have hugged and happily shared stories. My business partner's husband, when visiting, was kind but curt, attending only to business conversation. Looking back, I could have expressed what I had been thinking, but I had no interest in maintaining a relationship that would have been one-sided. Both of us could have benefitted from being empathetic to one another, and yet neither of us spent the time or effort. Our business relationship was also deteriorating, and both of us knew it. I felt that she wasn't going to understand or support that I was gay, or getting divorced.

It didn't take long for us to see that we really didn't want to work together. One day, my business partner said to me that she wanted to change her career path, and write books, and dedicate more time to the church. She said she was interested in selling her half of the clinic to me. Shocked with what she had said at first, it didn't surprise me, as I took notice of how our relationship had become strained. Nevertheless, I really didn't expect this big an upset, and I wasn't sure how I felt about it. When understanding what this might mean, I started to make lists of the pros and cons of being sole owner of the clinic. I sought the assistance of a lawyer who specializes in business acquisitions, to help me determine the fair market price of the clinic. I analysed my life, and wondered if I wanted to own the clinic or move into a different direction myself. While work was being done with my lawyer, accountant, and banker, I got closer to my answer. At first, I imagined that I would have liked to continue as the clinic owner.

As more time passed, my business partner saw that she had put fuel to the fire, to allow what she wanted: her separation from me. Unexpectedly, she wanted to bid for the clinic. When my partner and I had first opened the clinic, we had scheduled into our business agreement *The Shotgun Clause,* which helps to provide an exit provision with a buy sell agreement. I would've been happy owning the clinic, but even happier if I could sell it and move on to something totally new. To make a very long story short, my business partner and I negotiated the sale calmly and systematically, over the Internet. I happily sold my half of the business.

I was delighted to have been set free once again, as I sold my half of the clinic.

Dignified Divorce

I told myself a long time ago that I never wanted to divorce my husband. I told Him, when I *came out,* that I didn't want to get a divorce. During revealing conversations, I told Her, my therapist, my friends, and Carol that I didn't want to get a divorce. Then, to my surprise, but very sure of myself, I found myself sitting in my lawyer's office, where I announced that I wanted a fair and dignified divorce.

During my quiet times when I sat home alone in the living room, I would pan the room and imagine my life not living there and not married to my husband. I imagined my daughters having a different relationship with their mom and dad, while living in two homes. I knew that I would have to work even harder to assure my kids that their mom and dad loved them as much as they ever had, and that they would always be loved to the fullest. They would be living in two homes, but we would still be attending their school meetings and celebrations, and recognizing their accomplishments together as a family. I imagined how my living arrangements would change. We had accumulated and treasured more than 20 years of furniture and stuff, and things that would have to be divided up. I looked at the story-filled family heirlooms from our parents, and would get a sinking feeling in my stomach when thinking this familiar life of mine would change to something that I couldn't yet imagine. I questioned how I would feel doing that, and if I could pack up half my things and just go.

In my mind, I'd offer to be the one to move to another home, and not too far away from our marital home. Where would that be? Could our daughters continue at the same schools and after school programs, even when they lived in two homes? How would they and I adjust to that? My imagination and questions for hundreds of scenarios kept crowding my every thought. I only became more comfortable with the images when I saw the joyful endings, and I was determined to go forward and plan the next phase of my life with sincerity.

I assured my female lawyer that it was important to me to have a cordial, respectful, and cooperative divorce. I told her that I didn't plan on taking up too much of her time, or spending too much money on legal fees. I wanted to do as much of the work of organizing the children, and dividing the assets, that I could do on my own. My husband and I had agreed to share the children 50/50 with regards to time and expenses. We had liked the schedule that my husband had heard about when sharing children. It was the 5:2 Ratio. Dad parents the children Monday and Tuesday, and Mom parents Wednesday and Thursday; and the weekends—Friday, Saturday, and Sunday—are alternated. I liked the schedule because it gave each of us two consistent days where we would be responsible for the kids, and two days where we knew we could be on our own.

I told my lawyer that my husband and I should be able to come to a compromise with most decisions. My lawyer questioned if we would be able to work through an amicable divorce. She said it was rarely done, if ever. I thought then, while we were dutifully and politely finishing a job that could have created angry and bitter feelings, that we were going to be able to divorce with dignity. Of course, there were disagreements, and occasional feelings of unequal or unfair outcomes, and I'm sure that each one of us felt like we could have done better at times; but fortunately, we were able to separate our lives fairly, while keeping our own dignity intact, and our children feeling very loved and secure. To this day, He and I both stand behind each other in maintaining family unity and love.

I worked really hard focusing on love, to have one happy family, living under two roofs.

Pillars Crumble

The most stable pillars in my life, which I thought would have stood the test of time, had crumbled. I did realize that I started the changes by *coming out.* I may not have come out in a way that everyone would be accepting and pleased, but I'd have never thought that so many of my relationships would have been affected so strongly and, in the end, so completely destroyed. This process was all new to me, and everyone else too. I see that none of us knew how to proceed in a way where everyone was going to feel good, with no harm done. As I did my best to stand for what I believed in, I watched my long-time relationships end. My husband and I had separated, and our divorce papers had been served. My plans to move out, find a new home, and live on my own had begun. My children would take turns living with their father and me. My business relationship had ended, and I sold my physiotherapy clinic that I had founded. And I lost many of the connections that were associated with my marriage, my home, and my business. I even watched my relationship between my 30-year-old godson (my business partner's son) and me dwindle. I could have put more work into securing the bonds, but I was tired of being excluded by my business partner's family, and many others, and I was no longer interested. I didn't feel that my Godson, or other friends, were interested in maintaining a relationship with me at all. Their negative energy toward me wasn't good for me. It was sad, but I moved on.

To make matters more emotional, my heart and head were getting tugged at as my relationship with Her slowly started to drift apart. She hadn't just been my best friend and my soul mate for as long as I could remember, but I knew that She was hurting as she watched me change, and I wasn't there to support her. I became so busy with keeping my own family together, organizing my moving plans, and creating my new workplace, and my focus was on me. I regret my selfishness when looking back, and it's these times when I feel grateful that I've learned and grown from these experiences. Very determined, I soon started a new physiotherapy company: Get Better Physio.

As my attention centred on divorce lawyers, business lawyers, finding a new home, and caring for my children during wearisome times, I had little time to rest, and even less time for Her. When we were together, I loved how I felt so free when we were in our lesbian space, while dining and dancing in the gayborhood on the weekends. It wasn't as easy to see one another during the week because both of us were busy with our own lives. As time went on, I was moving forward, and although I thought that she wanted to enjoy a life with me, She wasn't making the changes I needed, when she knew that I wanted to live a real lesbian life—whatever that meant. She continued to tell me that she wasn't a lesbian, and that she didn't want to leave her husband. I sometimes felt a tension between us. I believed that she loved me, but she also loved her husband and wanted to remain with him. She and I had lived in our own love bubble of just us for so many years, and that was all we knew. At the same time, He and I lived in our family bubble of just us. I no longer wanted isolation, but I wanted open and deliberate living.

I loved both of them, and thought I could continue living a dual life, until the bubbles had burst open, and I had been set free of living 2 unconnected and very unbalanced lives. Without being able to explain it, I felt that being a lesbian was more than just being in love with "Her." I liked the real me, and how I felt being intentional, and knowing one day I would share my life with a woman.

Grateful for the Support

I looked forward to seeing Carol, more and more. Carol lived very close to me, so the convenience of a short, daytime visit together was easy. It was simple to go together to the gym to exercise, which I would have done on my own. We were able to go together to neighbourhood markets that I would have gone to on my own. Many of the events were lesbian events, and I would not have gone to those—and boy, would I have missed out. Carol would tell me that she had planned on going to a lesbian movie at the Inside Out LGBT film festival, and would ask if I would like to join her. At other times, she would say that there was an LGBT rally, in support and celebration of a high school boy who led the struggle to support same sex couples at his catholic school prom, and asked if I would like to go. The events were endless, and I became very involved in the LGBT community, very quickly.

To my surprise, co-facilitating a support group was the most therapeutic thing for me that I could have done. Carol had facilitated her own lesbian support group at a neighbourhood community centre for a couple of years. She always seemed to know what to say in answer to many of my *"what could I do if"* questions. She asked me to join her at the monthly (secretly known as the book club) meetings, and I was so glad I did. There would be between eight to fifteen women sitting comfortably on couches, in a circle, in the main room. Carol would begin each session by welcoming the women and reminding them that we were all in a safe, private space where we could speak freely what was in our hearts, knowing that we were being heard and would not be criticized, judged, or disrespected. Each woman would then speak for 2–3 minutes about her current issues. Familiar topics included *coming out* conversations with kids, negotiating divorce, to tell or not to tell senior parents, *coming out* at work, religious and ethnic difficulties, lesbian dating—and my favourite—planning field trips to socialize with the lesbians at dances and parties. The conversations were quite lively, with expressions of joy for *coming out,* or tears from the fears of the unknown. Often, the themes of anxiety and distress were repeated.

When a mother comes out to her kids, the children may think they are gay. The woman's spouse is often confused, and may show signs of sadness and anger. The women may resist telling their aging parents, not wanting to be responsible for resulting stressful illnesses. In extreme cases, women would fear for their own safety. In most cases, women found it extremely difficult to attend their very first meeting. At the end of the first meeting, many women would leave, relieved that they felt normal and not alone. They may have been going to therapy for years, but in just one support group session, when surrounded by many others in the same situation, they felt comforted and reassured that everything would work out.

Every night, there was laughter, and there were success stories. The situations shared most often demonstrated that loving communication and having patience during the *coming out* process, usually ended with improved family support. Each story was different, and I learned most from active listening and taking small steps, practicing the suggestions that seemed to work for others. *Coming out* seemed to be a full-time job/journey of its own, and a process that would be repeated often.

When coming out, I learned that all I could do was the best that I knew. Half of the people asked, "Why didn't you tell me sooner?" The other half asked, "Why did you have to tell me?" Now, I'm just me, and share my life like everyone else does, as it comes up naturally.

Chapter 8

How Will Your Kids Turn Out?

When is it the Right Time to Tell the Kids?

I focused on keeping together a normal, same old family life, even though I really didn't feel the same at all. The daily activities with my family didn't change, but what I thought about during the day-to-day activities was completely new. I was determined to keep my family life connected, while I was making plans on how to change my personal relationships. I really enjoyed spending time with Carol, who seemed to be happy with who she was. We would socialize with her lesbian (I had gotten more comfortable using the label) friends, and go to LGBTQ (Lesbian, Gay, Bisexual, Trans, Queer) movies and community events. I was learning so much about the struggles and the triumphs in the LGBTQ world. I listened to new music by LGBTQ singers. The lyrics in Melissa Etherege's songs replicated the stories of my own life. By listening to them, I was able to imagine how my life could strengthen, and where my life could lead. I was inspired, and excited, and although inexperienced, I was independent, and chose to stop the legacy of guilt and shame for being me.

During our lesbian support group meetings (2002–2014), a specific theme was sometimes chosen to discuss in detail. Most of the women had children, and all of the women were worried about how and when to tell their children that they were lesbian. The topic of children of lesbian moms was often a favourite because lesbian moms are afraid of losing their children's love, and even the connection to the family. The women's opinions on how and when to tell their children, varied. Many felt that they would wait to tell the kids, until they got older. The age of when they were *old enough* was often disputed. The intention of the discussions throughout the night was to share a story while the others just listened. This was therapeutic for the speaker, and educational for the group. As each of the women told their story, it was then up to the listeners to take the information and either decide to try it because it made sense in their lives, or learn never to repeat it.

When Sally told the group about her teenage son, we were all shocked and saddened. Following Sally's son knowing that his mother was a lesbian, he became angry and aggressive. When she would drive to pick up her son to take him to her house, her son would throw rocks at her car from his bedroom window, while swearing and screaming at her. She got reports from her ex-husband that her son was doing really poorly at school, and he had gotten arrested for vandalizing property at a golf course. The group discussion that night focused on pursuing a loving relationship, and getting professional family counselling.

Lori had been forbidden to visit with her infant grandchildren after she had *come out* to her adult daughter and son-in-law. To make matters worse for Lori, she was no longer invited to her grandchildren's celebrations, or to the family holiday celebrations. Lori was so distraught, and was at her wits end on what to do. At the end of the evening, we discussed the importance of educating the families of those *coming out,* and handed out pamphlets listing the meeting times from PFLAG (Parents and Friends of Lesbians and Gays), for additional resources.

I think that with continued, consistent loving attention, a strong support system, and dedicated listening skills while showing concerns for the children's needs, children of any age will grow to live happier, more honest, and fuller lives.

When the Time is Right

Each month, I sat alongside Carol in the support group meetings, listening so carefully, and learning from the other women's stories regarding their hesitations and fears of *coming out* to their children.

Leslie told us that when she shared her story with her two children, that her teenage daughter wondered if being lesbian was genetic. Her daughter stated that she was worried that she may be gay, and she'd be very upset and wouldn't want to be gay. Leslie had to review with her that so far, there was no evidence in current research that being gay is hereditary, and her daughter is no more likely to be a lesbian than anyone else in society.

When Vera told the group her story about the time she told her son, she explained that when she had finished telling him that she was a lesbian, he turned to her and shared that he was gay. They were both equally surprised, and would understand each other as they worked through their journeys together and separately.

The unfortunate situations can be very traumatic. Thankfully, these occurrences weren't common amongst our group, but we all took extra time to think and discuss scenarios to help improve our relationships with our children. We spoke of the risks and benefits, and I was getting ready to have my own *coming out* conversation with my daughters. I concentrated on the benefits, and knew that the best way for me to teach my children honesty (after feeling awful for keeping secrets for so many years) was to be honest with them myself. And if I could share my difficult stories with them, then I'd hope that they could come to me to share their difficult stores with me. Since their ages ranged from 8 years old to 17 years old, I understood that the content in the conversations would be very different.

Both the topics of *coming out* and divorce were very complex and hard issues to talk about with anyone, let alone my own children. I was comfortable, confident, and proud to be a lesbian, and wanted to send a positive message that unlike what kids may have heard in school, being gay isn't wrong, it isn't a sin, and it isn't bad. I wanted the story to be such that I was telling them because I wanted them to know that it is OK to be gay.

As I read more about how to *come out* to kids, I learned:

1. It's never too early, because kids understand love, and they love you.
2. It's never too late, because the truth will always be welcome.
3. Choose a quiet space so that the conversation is personal and confidential.
4. Repeat that your love and commitment will always be strong and supportive.
5. Reassure and show them that you are still you.
6. Be ready for many kinds of responses, ask questions, and listen carefully.
7. Know that this is a lifelong conversation, and full understanding could take time.
8. Make sure there is plenty of time for thought and more questions.
9. Friday or Saturday offers more rest time than Sunday, before the start of the week.
10. Respect your children's wishes on when and how they want to share your news.
11. Provide them with contacts to other supportive adults, who they can speak with.
12. Remind them that they're not alone, and many children have two moms.

I wanted to make the time right, for easy and comfortable conversations with my kids. Even though I wanted to tell them sooner rather than later, I waited for that special moment when I was ready.

"Are You a Lesbian, Mom?"

I had heard that children know much more than their parents realize. I didn't realize how much my daughter Nicole really suspected, or knew, until she surprised me. It was almost midnight, and she had just returned home from a trip to NYC, having visited family and friends. We were chatting while she was unpacking and getting ready for bed. I must have said something about Her, and Nicole said, "Are you a lesbian, mom?" Well, when I caught my breath, and calmed my nervous racing heart, I looked at her, and replied, "It's really late (I paused); you just got home from NYC (another pause), and I think it's better that we talk about this tomorrow." (A long pause.) Then, I said, "Go unpack a bit more, and think about whether you want to talk about this now. I'm going to the kitchen for a drink of water." I was the one that needed a time out. "If you still want to talk, I will talk tonight." I figured neither one of us would have slept at all anyways. Ten minutes later, Nicole returned, wanting to talk.

I was ready, and quickly figured out that I wanted to give truthful yet simple information, but in answer to her questions, and not much more. Nicole looked at me, and repeated her question, "Are you a lesbian, mom?" I looked softly back at her, and whispered a sweet reply of, "Yes." I then continued, and quietly spoke about how I had been a lesbian for a long time but didn't know what to do because I was married to her dad and had 3 children. I went on to say that I had told her dad, but I hadn't told many other people. I then added that I was now ready to stop the secret, and work on what to do next for the good of our family. Nicole asked if I would I be getting a divorce, and would we be moving? Wow, serious questions with complex answers, so I turned the question back to her, and asked, "Do you think we should get a divorce?" With little hesitation, she answered, "Yes, but could this wait until school is out for the summer, so I won't have to think much about it until then." I agreed, and went on to say that I thought about moving out, where my home would be close to her dad's, and the kids would live with both of us. I reminded her how much I loved her, and that we would always be a family. After Nicole asked a lot of questions, she quieted. We then hugged, and after, she said that she had nothing more to say; we both went to bed, and I called out, "I love you!"

It wasn't until after a few days—it could have been even weeks later—that Nicole came to me with an angry tone and harsh words, and told me that I should have never married her father, and I should never have had her. She said she hated her life, and she would never step foot into my new home. I had to tread very lightly here, for I knew from past experience when she would sometimes get upset and thrash out, that I must not rebuttal, defend, or argue. I was afraid of her words because these are the issues that tear families apart. I was determined to keep the family together, and show that we could, and would, be happy through life's challenges. I strongly felt that she needed to know that I loved her very much, and I would always love her, and that I would never regret that I had ever got married to her dad. I was always delighted to have her in my life, and we would always work together to show her our love.

From a young age, I planned and thought I knew how my life would go. Today, more than ever, I continue to experience things that surprise me. I do my best, and then learn that things could have been done differently, and often better. I learn so much from my children, and appreciate everything I learn.

"The Time is Right Now"

Having had the unexpected experience of revealing my secret to my eldest daughter, I was more ready to have a scheduled conversation with Tania, my 14- year-old. Since Tania is consistently sweet and even-tempered, and I had the tiny bit of experience from speaking with Nicole, I felt more relaxed and ready for a sharing conversation. I told Tania that there was something important that I wanted to talk to her about. We arranged a time to go to a coffee shop, and chat. Following the pleasantries, I told her that I was gay, since the word lesbian wasn't as commonly used. She looked at me, and said "OK." I looked back at her, and took note of the silence. Then, she looked at me, and I looked at her. She isn't overly expressive and, as we sat for a moment, I asked if she had anything to say, or any questions. She replied, "No." Then, I mentioned that I had told Nicole, who had some questions, and did she want to hear what her questions were? So, Tania said, "Sure."

From then on, we talked briefly about how things at home wouldn't be changing much right away, but that maybe, eventually, her dad and I might get divorced. She said, "OK." I wasn't sure if she was so deeply upset that she was speechless, or she wasn't really worried or upset at all. I emphasized how much I loved her, and that her dad and I would always be a family, just different. I told her that I was thinking that I may move out to a new home in the neighbourhood, and that she and her sisters would take turns living with both of us. When Tania seemed to be OK, I asked her if she would want to help me decorate and choose colours for her new bedroom. After she said, "Sure," we finished our drinks, and went home, and I thought to myself, "Well, that was easy." I later learned that she had thought I was going to tell her that I was ill, or had cancer. Wow, I really don't know what my kids are thinking until I ask.

I had decided early on that my story to my youngest daughter, Gabi, then 8 years old, was going to be different. On a sunny, spring day, I asked my daughter to go on a neighbourhood bike ride with me. We set off down the street, and after just 4 turns, about ½ km, I asked to stop in front of a group of townhouses to rest. We got off of our bikes, and sat on the curb in front of townhouse #16. While sitting close to one another, I told Gabi that I might move out of our house and move to this house. Gabi looked at me, and asked why. "Well," I continued, "Your dad and I don't want to live together anymore." She then asked why again, as kids do, and I replied, "We have grown apart, and have different interests." I tried to keep it simple. She didn't ask any more questions after that, and didn't appear to be upset or wondering what this all meant. I stressed that we both loved her and her sisters very, very much, and that our love wouldn't change. I said that she would continue at the same school, with the same friends, and she would still go to gymnastics and swimming lessons at the same YMCA. She listened without a lot of questioning. I told her that she would have 2 houses, and 2 bedrooms, and she could walk from house to house a lot. I didn't tell her about my being gay. It wasn't time. I then asked her if she would like to pick out her bedroom set, and choose the colour of her carpet. She replied, "Sure," and we agreed that we would work together designing and decorating her room. We then hugged, cycled home, and she helped me prepare the family dinner.

As I write this sequence of events, and review the conversations, it all seemed so straightforward and easy. And, well, it kind of was. There was back and forth, descriptive and kind conversation. There was no extra explaining to do. There was no anger, no upset, and no tears. And if there was, it was well hidden; I even looked.

"Moving Out When Coming Out"

All of the important critical changes that I was planning for could or should've upset and overwhelmed me, but they didn't, and instead, I felt relaxed and hopeful that I was headed to a more authentic and happier place and time. Besides that, I rarely felt bothered because I had envisioned these times. I had played them out in my mind, over and over, and over again. After living in my family home for 22 years, I was moving out to a nice rental townhouse close by. I had to pack up by myself, all of my personal things, the furniture, and each item that my husband and I had agreed that I would take with me. The collecting, sorting, and packing into boxes was mostly done when my husband was at work and the kids were at school. I tried so hard to minimize the fact that I was taking things out of the house. I'm sure everyone thought I was taking their things.

If you remember, I was an experienced packer, both with the details of the job, and the setting aside of everyone's unwanted emotions. My hidden shield went up, and I became focused and determined to close this chapter, and speed up this tricky and uncomfortable process. I tried not to make it too obvious that I was packing up my things to take away with me, but in fact it was really obvious and extremely complicated. I don't remember my kids around watching me, or asking me what I was doing. I packed quietly, and tried to be as inconspicuous as I could. This must have been weird or straining for my kids and Him, since the packing up was not just the job of putting items in boxes but the knowing that soon after the packing was finished, I wouldn't be living in that house anymore. I was completing a complicated job, all on my own, in front of everyone, without discussing it. I was pleased that I was moving forward, yet sad and anxious when I thought how He must have been feeling. Nothing was ever talked about, and I just figured that everyone was focused on themselves, and going about their day, just as I was trying to go about mine.

On moving day, my dear, lesbian friend, Kim, arrived at my home, and offered to help me. The moving van was filled with more than 100 numbered boxes, chairs, couches, and tables, and driven two blocks through the neighbourhood, and parked at my new townhouse. As the movers emptied the van, Kim and I helped them carry the heavy boxes up the stairs into the house. I noticed that Carol had already surprised me, having planted colourful welcoming flowers in the flowerbox on the front porch. The furniture store delivery truck with the new bedroom sets had also arrived. It was almost midnight when we had finally finished putting the furniture and boxes in their places. This was my first sleep in a new place, at the start of another chapter.

At this point, I was sad, but I knew it was best for me to have less conversation and connection with Her. She was my first lesbian love, exposing and giving me permission to be the real me. I was grateful for that, and I will never forget our deep bond and the wonderful way she made me feel, all those years. But it was time for me to move ahead, stop the heterosexual charade, and be on my own. I no longer wanted secrets and the worry about what people thought regarding my sexual identity. I didn't want to live under the microscope on whom I should love, or religious teachings on what is and is not a sin, or by the requests of Him or Her on who I should or shouldn't connect with, or what information I should or shouldn't share.

My fear of loss, my fear of being hurt, and my fear of hurting others were the main reasons why I didn't move forward in my life sooner. I was so ready to put away my fears, and welcome the present moment to create sincere joy and health.

"The Gaydy Bunch"
Here's the story of 2 lovely ladies, caring for 6 well-balanced kids

My ready to move in, spacious, three-bedroom plus den, rental townhouse was perfect. My daughters seemed to like it, and they were able to walk back and forth from my house to their dads, in ten minutes. I was happy to furnish my home with enough beds, furniture, and personal space for everyone, including extra guests. There was even a great open foyer for Tania to practice her cello lessons. The 50/50 parenting schedule was shared between Him and me, allowing us to have an equal number of days to be with the kids, and an equal number of days for each of us to concentrate on work, or personal activities of our own. At the beginning, there was a lot of juggling and multitasking with the new schedule, but as time went on, like most things, routines set in, and a sense of familiarity and comfort ensued. During times that items were forgotten at His house, or extra unexpected trips had to be made to His house, I'd go back and forth naturally, and made it seem like this was a part of normal life, knowing that it would be expected that the kids would sometimes be frustrated and bothered by living in two houses. I certainly appreciated when He and I worked as a team when organizing the driving to school, after school programs, and emergency doctor appointments.

Carol and I were spending a lot more time together now that I had a place of my own. I was in an "OMG, pinch me" moment, shocked that I was living and playing house in my new lesbian life that I had so often dreamed of. Carol would occasionally bring her daughter over while my daughters were with me for dinner, for an all girls' sleepover. Her two boys would sleep at their dads, but the family dinners were a great way for all of us to connect. I wouldn't be surprised if her sons felt outnumbered sitting with six females at the dinner table. Often, on the weekend, Carol's eldest son would sleep over to be closer to his girlfriend's house. Anyone, and everyone, was welcome to stay with us, for any reason, I always liked a house full of kids.

After Carol and I had known each other a year and a half, and I had been living on my own for six months, Carol moved in. She eased the transition for her kids and herself by visiting them often at the family home to give them lunch or spend time with them after school. Carol's husband had known, and nicely accepted that she was a lesbian, many years prior to us meeting. I'm sure her husband was very sad but graciously understood that one day they would separate if she were to fall in love with the right woman. Another six months quickly passed, and Carol and I were in love with each other and wanted to make a life together. We liked the neighbourhood and bought our own home down the street where we could live together and have a bed for each of our six kids. I was organizing, packing, renovating a house, and moving again, but this time I saw more permanence with my relationship and my life. I was especially happy when I could confidently say, "Our kids are alright." My daughters were often exposed to their LGBTQ friends and teachers at their arts school, and they would entertain their friends at our house. It was nice when, one year, Tania and her boyfriend pitched in to help us make pride parade signs, and the next year, Nicole marched with us in the pride parade with her boyfriend. There were many indicators that the kids supported us, and compromised and adjusted to our new life the best they could.

February 14, 2005, was our first day in our new home. While getting ready for school, Carol and I had a kitchen full of kids during our first Valentine's Day breakfast together. The heart shaped plates and bright red napkins set the perfect scene for a perfect day, full of love. At 7:30am, the telephone rang, and Carol was told by her brother that her 84-year-old father had peacefully passed away that morning while in his room at the nursing home. A very sad Happy Valentine's Day!

Chapter 9

Born This Way

Starting a "Lesbian Family Lifestyle" at 45

At 84 years old, Carol's father's passing wasn't a tragedy but certainly not expected, and oh, so sad. Of course, he was loved, and would be missed. I knew I faced the responsibility, as Carol's life partner, to show her and her mother, family, and friends, my loving support. I also knew that her husband of 25 years would be present at the funeral and viewings. I wasn't an established member of this family but felt quickly put to the test to fit in. I was familiar with sitting Shiva (period of 7 days of formal mourning for the dead in the Jewish religion) but had never been on the inside as a part of the family. I'm Armenian to start, but often because of my many Jewish friends and connections, I've sometimes referred to myself as being Jew-ish. During the Shiva, I had some quiet moments to think. The Jewish religious narrative was totally different from what I'd known, and yet the many parts of this scenario were no different from what I'd done before. And I was determined to show that my *lesbian lifestyle* was simply a life of two women who loved each other, and were dedicated to each other as a couple. With my three children, I now lived with a woman who had three children, and was a member of a Jewish family, and I was sitting Shiva with my new family. This was an authentic me, being a lesbian, and being introduced to Carol's family as her partner. So many of my new experiences and feelings at that time were unfamiliar, and often uncomfortable. But as I became more practiced in my new relationships, I usually felt liberated, lived deliberately and proudly, and felt completely fulfilled.

In the beginning days, my eldest daughter had decided that she'd continue to live with her dad full time, and visit us often, and sleep over once in awhile. My other two daughters would continue with the 50/50 schedule that had been working for us. Carol's kids would go back and forth between their two homes, and continue with the arrangement that had worked for them. We had enough beds and space for the kid's stuff, and room for anyone who wanted to stay overnight. I loved when the kids slept over, and when they brought their friends. A modern, blended family paints a very nice picture. If I wanted to enjoy my life's journey within this family, I had to work hard to communicate, compromise, and practice lots of patience when dealing with the inevitable family drama, especially with 6 females living together in the same house, where four of them were from the ages of 10–19 years old. In the beginning, we enjoyed a lot of really good times, but it wasn't always pretty. There were more difficult moments when the kids acted like kids, and became upset or got emotional. Gladly, most of the time, unlike the worrisome stories that we hear about, our family conflicts were open to discussion, and resolved. I learned when to speak out, when to listen carefully, when to pause, and when to keep completely quiet.

I cherished setting up our neighbourhood house together, with everyone taking part. I was experiencing another *pinch me moment,* feeling ecstatic that I was entering a life that I had dreamed of for so long. I was gratefully healthy, loved my female partner and our new family, was still excited to wake up and treat my patients, and enjoyed my many, many new friends. I wanted everyone to know that my living with a woman, and raising a family, was almost the same as my living with a man and raising a family. What is so wrong with this lesbian lifestyle?

Being partnered with a woman, and living a loving family life, was to be my "Lesbian Family Lifestyle;" after all, it's love that makes a family.

It's Not Easy Being Gay

I could never have predicted the range of consequences I would face when coming out as part of the LGBTQ community. I'd heard that gays were discriminated against, and that many people interpreted that the bible considered homosexuality a sin, but I had no idea the extent of the suffering. There were the shattered lives, the broken families, the physical, emotional, and social abuses, the illnesses, and the horrible suicides. I never knew, until I experienced the discrimination myself, and noticed my friendships deteriorating, and some of my social circles disappearing. Now, I understood that some of the changes in my friendships were due to my divorcing my husband. And I realized that people take sides, and when people feel awkward, they avoid conversation and contact. But even though I had my friends while I was part of a couple, I was sad when my girlfriends didn't attempt to understand my situation, or make an effort to continue our friendship. In one instance, I invited a few of my Armenian girlfriends to my home for an afternoon get-together. One of them said that her husband said that she couldn't come over because I was a bad influence. We had been friends for more than 15 years. I was astounded, upset, and sad. That afternoon, instead of meeting at my house, we all went to a coffee shop to be together. I don't remember what we talked about, but that was almost 20 years ago, and I haven't socialized with any of them since. There are so many reasons for friendships, and I guess they just didn't like me as much as I thought or hoped they did. That will be another book one day, on *Understanding Friendships.*

People Do Not Choose to be LGBTQ, They Just Are LGBTQ

No one would just choose to be a part of the LGBTQ community. If there's a choice to be made, it's that people choose to be who they were born to be. And who better to decide this than the people themselves. It's well known that LGBTQ people are more likely to experience intolerance, discrimination, harassment, and the threat of violence when compared to the heterosexual population. And as time went on, and I became immersed in the gay community, I felt an anger brewing inside me as I witnessed for myself, and heard story after story in my support group, in the media, and on the Internet, the negativity, anger and insulting exclusion.

As an example, just one month following my divorce, when I had moved out on my own, sadly, my 80-year-old mother-in-law, Araxie, passed away. I had respected and loved her deeply, for over 20 years. While struggling with my own sadness, I maintained my composure so that I could support my daughters, who I knew would be devastated. I wanted to be there for my husband as well, if he wanted me to help. On the day of the funeral, I had heard that my sister-in-law thought it would be better if I didn't attend the funeral, since I was no longer a part of the family. Well, I was furious, and told my sister-in-law that this had absolutely nothing to do with her at all, but that I loved my mother-in-law, and needed to be at her funeral for myself and my children.

This was the first of many stabs when I searched hard to find ways on how to stay positive. I wondered why I was being totally cut off and excluded, over and over. Was it because I had been divorced, or because I was lesbian, or some other reason? Fortunately, Michelle, a dear friend of my mother-in- law, had heard that I wasn't being included in the family limousine or at the family luncheon table following the church service, so she called me and told me that she would pick me up, and we would drive together to the services. I'm sure my mother-in-law's love for me sent Michelle to me that day. I was so grateful for her kindness and consideration. Just before the final arrangements, my husband redesigned the luncheon tables so that my husband, daughters, and I would sit together. All kinds of love make a family.

I strived to continue with traditional family activities we had done for years. One wintery Sunday, I took my three daughters to our Armenian church. After parking, the four of us walked on the snowy sidewalk toward the church entrance. At the same time, I noticed my very close friend was also walking on the same sidewalk, and as soon as she saw me, she made a sharp turn and began to run in her high heels, across the slippery parking lot, to avoid me. My daughters were so surprised to see her running, and asked why my friend suddenly ran across the parking lot in the wrong direction, and didn't stop to say hello. I shrugged my shoulders, and said that I didn't know. I thought to myself that I suspected she was running away to avoid me.

During a very wearisome time, one of my dear, gay friends told me that he was denied hospital visitation when his partner had been admitted to the emergency room following an injury. He had been asked to leave his partner's side, and sit and wait in the waiting room. That same friend wasn't invited to his partner's home for Christmas dinner that year. I've heard story after story, when friends of mine had lost their jobs, or lost their straight friends, or couldn't adopt children because they were gay. I've also heard the stories of the LGBTQ teachers and coaches, and aunts and uncles who were frequently looked upon with suspicion, while former spouses, parents, and families were often judged and ridiculed. Even some children of LGBTQ families were bullied and discriminated against. When will this discrimination stop? I really appreciated my long-time friends who asked me questions, were non-judgemental, and remained open to listening, learning, and understanding the stories that were unfamiliar to them. Better yet, they demonstrated compassion, concern, and continued support when they took the time, listened, and heard my story. They are my true friends.

I look forward to an all accepting and loving world, when "I love her; he loves him; and love makes a family," is the norm.

LGBTQ Trailblazers

I was a young adult in the 1980s and 1990s, while living a straight life. In love with Her, I kept a low profile, never exposing myself to anything regarding the LGBTQ world. While living in my bubble, the LGBTQ world was completely unknown to me. I had no idea that an LGBTQ community even existed, or that I could've learned about it or be exposed to it. I'd never even known, and was shocked to learn that there were small gay pride gatherings in the early 1980s, and bigger Pride Parades in the 1990s. It was only in the early 2000s when my suppressed love for Her was taken over by unhappiness and conscious thought, where my feelings became more than just love. The feelings I had, became a part of who I was, and directed my needs to understand and identify as lesbian. My eyes were opened, and I was ready to receive and see anything and everything to do with homosexuality, which I quickly learned and referred to as LGBTTQ (Lesbian, Gay, Bisexual, Transsexual, Two Spirited, Queer). I was then very interested in knowing about the true trailblazers who were changing the landscape of the mainstream cultures.

LGBTQ history dates back to ancient civilizations all around the world. It has only appeared in mainstream cultures in the last couple of decades, and is recorded in Wikipedia (https://en.wikipedia.org/wiki/Timeline_of_LGBT_history_in_Can ada).

During the 1600s, 1700s, and 1800s, the few documented LGBTQ notable events that occurred, involved people viewed as scandalise. Some were forced to resign from their jobs, or at worst, sentenced to death. But since the start of the 1900s, the narrative has changed, primarily due to the LGBTQ and human rights advocate trailblazers. With increased interest and ease when viewing international media, and the invention and rapid development of the Internet and cell phones, exposure to LGBTQ information was now easy to attain. It wasn't until as recently as 2001, when the Netherlands was the first country to allow same sex marriage. Then, in 2003, Belgium followed. In 2005, Spain allowed same sex marriage, and within the same year, Canada enacted the civil marriage act, also legalizing same sex marriage. Most recently, in 2017, gay marriage became law in Australia.

I'm pleased to say that I've had the honour of participating in many services at the Metropolitan Community Church of Toronto, while the senior Pastor, Reverend Brent Hawkes, delivers his insightful sermon at Sunday service. Rev. Hawkes is one of Canada's greatest champions for equal rights, and has been at the forefront of LGBTQ ministry in Toronto.

My early days of *coming out* started in the year 2000, when unknowingly, I was perhaps given permission by celebrities, the media, and modern day society to admit to myself that I was a lesbian. I often felt so blessed when I noticed my once closed doors opening right up, and making it easy for me to move forward with my own human rights. While living in Toronto, Canada, I've usually felt safe and supported within the LGBTQ community. I've learned that the coming out process is a lifelong process, and I'm grateful to the courageous pioneers who have proceeded me, and who had worked hard, making my coming out process safer and easier than it's ever been. I was reminded what a wonderful life I've had, when I was out to breakfast with two of my daughters, many years before I had had the conversation with my youngest.

While at a restaurant in the gayborhood, my youngest daughter, Gabi, noticed the rainbow flag (the LGBTQ symbol), and asked me why there was a rainbow flag. I turned to her older sister, Tania, and asked if this would be a good time to talk about kids having 2 moms. Tania smiled, and nodded her head in agreement. So, I said to Gabi, "Well, you know how there is a Canadian flag and an American flag, and an Armenian Flag, which we are proud to say is *our flag*? And you know how mom and Carol love each other, and we are all a family and live together? Well, the rainbow flag is a flag to show a family with two moms that live together with their children, as a family, or two dads that live together with children, as a family." Before I could say another word, Gabi nodded, and said, "Oh, I see; can you please pass the syrup?" Out of the mouths of babes; there was no judgement, and this topic had become a normal, familiar non-issue.

This normal, non-issue scenario comforted, encouraged, and prompted me to act.

While learning from my new lesbian friends what they had endured, and how they had marched in parades and lobbied to their politicians, I realized it was my time to step up to the plate. I had important messages, and needed to be an advocate. I wanted to walk through my day, proud of being a normal person/lesbian. I didn't only need to *come out*; I needed to just *be out*. So, for instance, during my socializing, I would take Carol to the Armenian Church picnic, or the Christmas service, or the Lenten luncheon, or the annual dance. Carol danced beautifully and effortlessly with the group of ladies, quickly picking up the steps that were so similar to her Israeli dancing. The congregation was being exposed to, and getting used to seeing us together as a couple at the different functions. The few people that turned the other way to avoid eye contact and pleasantries, still turned away, but most of the people turned toward us, smiled, and greeted us with a hug. I noticed that the people at church were more comfortable in my presence as they saw my efforts to demonstrate that I was a loving person, and how my life style was the same as theirs. I know that no loving God would deny the love of two consenting adults.

LGBTQ Myth Busters and Alternative Facts: True or False?

I'm pleased to be a proud and *out* lesbian. But that's not all. I also consider myself to be a joyful and healthy, devoted, same-sex partner. I'm a concerned ex-wife, and a loving mother, warm-hearted step-mother, soulmate sister, dependable step-daughter, reliable friend, helpful neighbour, caring physiotherapist, and committed citizen of the world, while being faithful and spiritual.

Can being a lesbian be such a bad thing? I know that my being a lesbian is the right thing. I also know there are widespread stories about the LGBTQ that are repeated over and over, so much so that they are believed.

People choose to be LGBTQ – False.
When do straight people choose to be straight?
Left-handed kids don't choose to be left-handed but choose what feels right.
Tomboys don't choose to be lesbians; lesbians are lesbians.
I didn't choose to be a lesbian. I chose to be me, a lesbian, and to live an honest life.

LGBTQ parents will raise kids to be LGBTQ – False
Straight parents raise 90% of LGBTQ people. Time has shown that kids cannot be taught or convinced to be straight or LGBTQ.
A child's chances of being LGBTQ are the same, whether LGBTQ or heterosexual parents raise them. Straight parents raised me. Straight parents raised my partner.
Carol and I have raised six kids, and they are all straight.

LGBTQ relationships don't last – False
Research has found this to be untrue. Long-term studies of LGBTQ relationships show that their relationships are the same as the straight ones. Evidence shows that most LGBTQ want to be in committed, long-term relationships, and are successful in doing so, despite the difficulties of social prejudice.
I have lived in a committed relationship with my partner, Carol, for over 15 years.

Same-sex couples' parenting skills aren't as good as with a mother and father – False
Studies have looked at teens, and have showed that their grades were similar in families with same gender parents compared to their counterparts in heterosexual homes. The same studies showed that the teens were no more likely to engage in troublesome behaviours. In summary, science shows that kids raised by same gender parents do as well as those raised by different gender parents.

LGBTQ have a definite unique alternative lifestyle – False
There is no definable LGBTQ lifestyle, just as there is no definable heterosexual lifestyle. Some people like to think that the *normal average lifestyle* is that of a heterosexual couple with two children—and, of course, a dog. In fact, less than 1/3 of all western families consist of a mother, father, and two children living in the same household. Within all communities, individuals create their own lifestyles.

The majority of paedophiles are LGBTQ – False
Depicting gay men as a threat to children may be the strongest weapon for provoking fears about homosexuality. In fact, a child is over 100 times more likely to be sexually assaulted by a heterosexual relative than an LGBTQ person.

History shows us that the LGBTQ are everywhere. They are of all ages, all cultures, all ethnic groups, and all religions. The causes of sexuality are unknown, and it isn't the cause that is important but that all people are treated with dignity and respect, regardless of their sexual orientation.

Homosexuality and Religion

I was frozen by fear for over 20 years, and powerless to admit to anyone around me, or even to myself, that I was homosexual. Regrettably, my fears kept returning to me as I kept hearing far too many stories of people in our society discriminating against people who were different, especially toward the LGBTQ. I really didn't feel different, so I didn't understand, but regardless, the fear continued to paralyze me. We are all, simply, people. And it's well known, that throughout history, people have found a way to use religion, and the Bible, as an excuse to hate, ridicule, ostracize, and persecute homosexuals. I certainly didn't want to hear from my church or Armenian community that I was sinning; while, in fact, I was loving, caring for, and truly honouring my lifetime partner.

Around the world, public opinion about homosexuality varies tremendously, while the issues of homosexuality and religion are considered one of the most divisive topics of today. Just as there are countless diverse religions and belief systems, there are also countless different religious outlooks on homosexuality. Religion is such a strong focal point in each society around the world, that it's been shown that regular personal participation in organized religion has proven to be the strongest predictor of whether a person disapproves of homosexuality or not. In addition, the status of inclusion of the LGBTQ people, within the communities of faith, continues to be a question of debate. This divisiveness often drives a wedge between those LGBTQ people wanting to keep their faith, and their choices of where they are welcome to worship. Fortunately, some progress is being made as the relationship between sexuality and religion continues to evolve. LGBTQ people are realizing that they don't have to choose between their faith and their sexuality.

Rather than review the contentious detailed history of religion's relationship with homosexuality, which can be better found in the thousands upon thousands of books and in social media, I just want it known how I have observed all types of people, in the name of religion, to silence and paralyze the LGBTQ community from speaking out or coming out. As astonishing as this may sound, I've spoken to religious right wing Christian neighbours who have admitted to me that they'd rather their child commit suicide than live their life in sin. We've been debating and discussing these issues for more than ten years. These same people continue to tell me that they love me. They've often asked for my opinions, and appreciate my suggestions on physiotherapy exercises, but they'll never support or approve of my living with a woman as my partner. I have my own opinions as to why they say the things they say, and I wonder how much of it is their truth, and how much of it is speaking in fear, to the ears of God. I carry on and continue to demonstrate my sincere kindness and generous gestures as evidence in showing my Christian, Canadian, Armenian, lesbian lifestyle of love. (This sounds like the making of a movie.)

I know, for a fact, that God only wants me to be honest and honourable, and He knows that I am. I know for a fact that God wants me to be fair and sensible, and He knows that I am. And I know that God wants me to live the life that I truly believe to be right for me. And I know, for a fact, that God only teaches love, and he loves me. And if you think differently, and you may, I know for a fact that God is the reason I am who I am, and that I have learned from God to live the best loving life for me.

Advocates for Change

**For more ways on how you can advocate see:
www.straighttogaybook.com**

While living in Toronto, Canada, it's become obvious to me that many religious and political leaders recognize that times are changing with regards to cultural attitudes about sexuality. And when attitudes change, behaviours, actions, and laws follow suit. But I know that doesn't mean that the majority fully embrace the shifts. Change can't happen overnight, and it'll take many of us to join in on the process, in order to really see the changes. I feel inspired, and hope for continuing change when I see that same-sex marriage is permitted in Canada, Belgium, Spain, and the Netherlands, to name just a few countries. But on the other hand, I'm angry and disheartened, and know that continued hard work is needed, when noting that homosexuality is illegal, and gay marriage is unthinkable in most African, Middle Eastern, and Asian nations.

I'm most proud of our freedom fighters, who have been *coming out*, year after year, in the struggle to improve the acceptance of sexual freedom in our society. I am so passionate, and walk the talk as an activist, to work for LGBTQ equality. I am noticed by the press who are ready to hear the LGBTQ messages and cries for equal rights. My children helped make my signs—2 lesbian moms, 2 straight dads, 6 kids, Love Makes a Family—and marched beside me in the Pride Parade. My children have become advocates alongside me.

For twelve years, I co-facilitated a lesbian support group, with my partner Carol. Together, we have often lead and marched in the Toronto Pride Parade. Customarily, the parade has between 6,000 and 8,000 LGBTQ participants, and it has been known to have 1.5–2 million people watching and supporting, alongside the parade route. We've also marched in The Dyke March, each year, and in the smaller town Pride Parades, surrounding Toronto. I've participated in, been interviewed, and photographed often by the media, as seen below:

June 2005 – The Toronto Star: The parade remains a voice for political activism as these parents showed last year – placards read: Love Makes a Family; 2 Moms + 6 kids + Love = 1 Happy Family; I am your physiotherapist; I am your neighbour; I am your friend.

March 2006 – The Toronto Sun
Unmasked: Lesbians celebrating *The right to be Me* International Woman's Day

July 2006 – Xtra Magazine
Reasons to March: We march for joy, For those who can't, To end the Hate.
I helped spearhead and design the float for The Metropolitan Community Church of Toronto, which won the award for *Most Fabulous Float*. Toronto's Pride 2006

June 2007 – Toronto 24 Hours
Pride Alive, in celebration of Pride Toronto, Teach Kids it's OK to be Gay

June 2008 – The Toronto Star
Marchers Dressed for Excess
Dyke March participants make strong political statement, with in-your-face attire

September 2010 – The Toronto Star
Late Blooming Lesbians find different kind of partnership
Soon after this article was published, Carol and I received many calls, or shall I say cries for help. So many women wanted to join our support group (more than doubling our attendance) that we had to break out into 2 groups of 15 women, in different rooms of our home, for several months. We still get the occasional call today, 7 years later, from women who have read the 2010 article online, and would like information or support on coming out.
https://www.thestar.com/life/health_wellness/2010/09/01/late blooming_lesbians_find_different_kind_of_love.html

August 2013 – IN Magazine Putting the Camp back into the Gay

January 2014 – HERSHE Magazine – Community Ambassador for World Pride
file:///Users/audreykouyoumdjian/Documents/Audrey/MISC/HerShe%20Magazine%20-%20Feature.webarchive

July 2016 – The Toronto Star
Pride Toronto: You Can Sit With Us, Invite him and his boyfriend to dinner

July 2017 – The Toronto Star, The Canadian Press
Toronto Dyke March, Toronto Police should March with Pride

July 2017 – Television News, CP 24, CTV, The Canadian Press
First Responders Unity Festival in support of the Police and all First Responders

Chapter 10

Conscious Living for Joy and Health

Creating your Future: You Be the Driver

You are the only one who creates in your experience—no one else. Everything that comes to you comes by the power of your thought. If there are changes you would like to make, it will be of great value to begin telling a different story—not only about your body, but about all subjects that have been troubling to you. As you begin to positively focus, getting to feel so good about so many subjects, you will begin to feel the power that creates worlds flowing through you.
Abraham Excerpted from the book, "The Law of Attraction": Learning to Attract Health, Wealth, and Happiness" #666

To feel happy, it's most important for me to be healthy, have positive relationships, feel abundance in all parts of my life, and to have meaningful experiences. Many believe that there are no coincidences. Evidence supports that 90% of your actions are under your control. That means you are in control of most of your day. Further evidence reported by the Centre for Disease Control states that 85% of all diseases are influenced by your emotions. These numbers indicate that if you can take control of your thoughts, emotions, and actions, you take control of your health and your life's path. I know I want the rest of my life to be the best of my life, and I know there's a myriad of things I can control and must do to live my best life. My life is a work in progress, and it's mine to create.

The good news here, for you, is that you already know all the rules, and I bet you could write your own books on what to do to be healthy, how to form relationships, and ways to spend less and save more. Follow the endless lists you've made on what to do and what not to do, and when you do it all perfectly, then you'll be happy. But following the lists alone doesn't work. Unfortunately, not many live the joyful healthy lifestyle they want. The best way to connect to joy is to be conscious, and to imagine and feel your way through each moment toward your desires. Being aware of your feelings during your day allows you to direct yourself towards good feeling moments. Feeling good, and following your desire, is calming, and reduces your stress. Being conscious means being aware of each and every one of your senses, to ground you in your moment in time. Being conscious means you are fully aware and in control of that moment. Turn your attention in the moment to how strong, safe, and stable you feel, and all the good that you see, that you hear, taste, etc., and be grateful for experiencing it. Be aware of each breath. With each grateful moment, you'll experience your smile erupting, while your feelings explode into joy. This is a good time to stay quiet and hold those feelings for as long as you can.

With practice, your ability to find and hold those joyous feelings will get so frequent that you'll get excited each time you travel to your conscious, joyous thought place. Controlling your feelings of joy will be so automatic, and will become your frequent default, so that you'll regularly be flooded with feelings of joy. When distress offsets joy, pause and reset. Take three breaths, be aware, and count the happy, positive parts of your entire surroundings. Your internal feelings of joy will return again. Notice once more all the things that prompt your feelings of joy. The fresh thoughts may help you to view things differently in the new moment, with a new perspective on the positive.

Each moment in my life is new, and I can create the outcome by consciously moving toward my desire for joy, thus improving the way I feel physically and emotionally.

The Law of Attraction – *When the student is ready, the teacher appears*

We are all Vibrational Beings. You're like a receiving mechanism, that when you set your tuner to the station, you're going to hear what's playing. Whatever you are focused upon is the way you set your tuner, and when you focus there for as little as 17 seconds, you activate that vibration within you. Once you activate a vibration within you, **Law of Attraction** *begins responding to that vibration, and you're off and running—whether it's something wanted or unwanted.*
Excerpted from North Los Angeles, CA – Sunday, August 18th, 2002
Our Love, Esther (and Abraham and Jerry)

For those of you who connect with the excerpt above, and if it speaks to you, please research the following:

* http://www.thelawofattraction.com/
* http://www.abrahamhicks.com/lawofattractionsource/ askitisgiven.php , and http://www.thesecret.tv/
* http://www.oprah.com/spirit/the-law-of-attraction-real-life-stories_1#ixzz4mjcd4AyX

Ten years ago, I read this excerpt (above), and thought it was an excellent explanation for the Law of Attraction, and one that made so much sense to me. I have since read the book, *Ask and It is Given*, by Esther and Jerry Hicks, and followed the messages of Abraham. I've seen *The Secret*, and I've become a strong believer in the concept that every thought I think, and the way that I feel, and what I do, is going to come back to me. I focus on the things I want to create for myself, and I use the Law of Attraction to manifest what I want, every day in my life.

Back in 1984, somehow, I had the feeling that I had to frame my diagnosis of M.S. in such a way that it wasn't going to be a part of my life. I didn't repeat the words, research the medical data, or discuss it with anyone. I repeated to myself that I was feeling healthy and strong, and would continue playing sports. I saw my plan to have children and open a physiotherapy practice. My thoughts were focused on health, and I acted in every way that I could to be healthy. Since becoming a committed reader and follower of the Law of Attraction, my life has opened to the world of abundance, through Ask, Believe, and Receive. While I lived for 22 years in a closet of guilt and fear, I continued to be grateful and appreciate all that was good in my life, and demonstrated positive joy, even during complications and heartache. I didn't know I had a choice to make a change. But it wasn't until my life was so threatened, and almost ended in the emergency room, that I needed to focus on being me, and realize that it was time to be courageous, overcome my fears, become authentic, and reveal the truth that I wanted to live my life honestly. As my unwanted thoughts shifted from hiding my life, to new desires of an open, sincere life, my point of attention shifted to joy, resulting in saving my life. My alarms go off when my health fails, indicating it's time for me to realign my emotions toward that of feeling good.

7 Steps to Strengthen the Law of Attraction

1. Relax and open your mind, and meditate (ponder, reflect) for just a few minutes.
2. Have a clear and detailed image of exactly what you want.
3. Send the Universe a mental picture of exactly what you want.
4. Write or draw, or picture your wish, and feel it happening to you.
5. Express your gratitude by recording all the things the Universe has given you.

6. Postulate (presume), be patient, don't ask how or when, and trust the Universe.
7. Watch for, welcome, and receive, as what you want comes into your existence.

The Ideal Lifestyle

You have your hand on the switch. You are the allower, or the resister. And your emotions tell you which one you are right now. It's easy, once you understand the formula: when you feel good, you're allowing good. When you don't feel good, you are not allowing good. We didn't say that when you feel good, you are allowing good, and when you feel bad, you are allowing bad (although it may translate into your experience in that way). There is only a Source of Well-being, which you are allowing or not.
Excerpted from the workshop in Ashland, OR on Saturday, July 20th, 2002 #717 – Abraham

For 40 years, I've been treating patients who have debilitating diseases, have been in devastating car crashes, have suffered disabling sports injuries, sustained agonizing burns, and who were deconditioned with chronic ailments. I never tired of hearing their complaints or cries of pain. I listened empathetically, acknowledged their feelings, treated their afflictions, and then stood strongly in a place of gratitude, and counted my blessings, literally. At the end of each day, I listed everything that was going right for me. And every time I stepped into my car to drive somewhere, I started my journey by first saying thankful words of gratitude: I can drive; I'm a good driver; and I'm fortunate that I own a car. I drove each day, giving my full attention, as if I'd been given another chance at driving and getting safely to my destination. Why am I saying this here? Because I've lived my life being exposed to the ills of people, and when I do meet and treat patients today, who have lived full lives to the age of 80 or 90 or older, I have asked them how they got to be old. I've gone on to say that I wanted to be just like them when I grow up, and I was interested to learn everything that they did right. From their comments, and from my readings, I've put together the lifestyle that I follow. Maybe this will be the design of the lesbian lifestyle.

Ten Strategies: Creating Joy and Health

For more health tips see:
www.straighttogaybook.com

1. **Feed Your Body Healthy Food:** Your best medicine is in the grocery store, not the pharmacy.
2. **Exercise to Strengthen Your Body and Lift Your Mood:** dance, walk, garden, and swim. Movement and exercise reduces the need for medication, surgery, and psychiatry.
3. **Pause, Rest, Relax, Pray, and Be Aware, to focus on joy and treasure each moment.** Quiet your mind, and view your surroundings to calm your mood and see the positive.
4. **Maintain a Regular Sleeping Schedule in a Bedroom that is Quiet, Dark, and Tranquil.** Melatonin (natural hormone) is released, and helps reduce inflammation; the spine elongates; the heart rate and blood pressure decreases; muscles repair; growth, and maintenance occurs; and the immune system works overtime to fight infection and disease.
5. **Work or Volunteer to Feel Accomplished and Worthy.** Meet new people, gain new skills, and feel proud about making a difference.
6. **Connect with People and Pets for Social Bonding and the Feeling of Connectedness.** Experience love and compassion, less anxiety and depression, higher self-esteem and empathy, improved immunity, and 50% increased chance of longevity.
7. **Pursue, Study, and Learn New Skills:** activities, interests, hobbies, and languages, for self-improvement and personal growth.
8. **Play, Laugh, and Have Fun:** join a club, visit the zoo.

9. **Travel Far Away or to a Neighbouring Town:** break from routine to wind down.
10. **Get Outside in Nature for Healthy Sun Exposure, and to Breathe With the Trees:** it's no joke when I say stop and smell the roses.

People don't understand that well-being is always the natural state. Your state of health is not taken away because you smoked, or you ate the wrong food or too much food, or drank too much alcohol, didn't exercise, exercised too much, or were in a car crash. Your state of health and well-being will only continue from your desire and thoughts focusing on your good health. Once you focus on your desire to feel good, intentions to do well, and to be healthy, and your thoughts consistently point to healthy, you will automatically be healthy—if your inner feelings, thoughts, and actions are in sync.

Move Better, Feel Better, Get Better Physio (Exercise is the best medicine)

For more information on physiotherapy, creating Joy and health see: www.straighttogaybook.com

"If it's Physical, It's Therapy." That was the saying on my University of Toronto T-shirt, back in 1977. I still stand by it today, 40 years later, as a passionate physical therapist, or as we say in Canada, physiotherapist. As I reflect back, I still remember when I stood in my clinic during a meeting in 2005, when I surprisingly heard myself tell my staff that I would be selling my half of the company, and moving on toward new physio endeavours. From surprised to nervously delighted, I soon noticed opportunities open up for me to establish a new physiotherapy practice that would free up my life, and assist the many patients that were unable to travel to a clinic. I would provide physiotherapy treatment for patients, right in their own homes. My partner, Carol, encouraged me, and came up with the genius name, *Get Better Physio*, which I thought was perfect. We attached the slogan: Move Better, Feel Better, Get Better, which I thought nicely summarized my core beliefs and the benefits of the treatment. Then, while counting on the experience within my head, in my hands, and through my heart and soul, I was ready to go from home to home, providing *Get Better Physio*.

My family, true friends, dedicated patients, and long time colleagues knew that I had changed my professional direction, and had moved on to provide in-home treatment, professional training, wellness consulting, and inspirational public speaking. Before long, my new practice supported a diversified clientele and new job tasks, which challenge me still, and keep me excited to go to work each day. I look forward to treating my patients, and they tell me that they look forward to my arrival. They often say that they enjoy the exercises we do together, the things they learn, the confident yet gently touch of my hands, my inspiring coaching, the improvements they see, and the way they feel when I leave their home. I may treat a patient once, to provide pre-op education, and an exercise program that they agree to continue on their own. Or, I may treat a patient fifteen times, following a hip replacement, to improve strength and function. Once I've treated a patient, I'm often called back to treat them for a different injury/impairment, or to treat their family members or a friend.

I welcome the new opportunities when I'm contacted. I assist clinic owners with the management of their practices when needed. I fill in for physios when emergencies come up, and provide consulting, education, and training to newly hired staff. I have become available when openings have come up for teaching positions, clinical evaluations, and academic testing. Companies request my consulting skills when neck and back care education is needed for their employees. The list of new possibilities goes on, and my enthusiasm to take on new challenges grows.

I feel forever grateful to have found a profession that fills me each day with continuous learning, stimulating challenge, and vital purpose. To complete my abundant life, I'm totally surrounded by kind and appreciative people who share in my life of joy and laughter.

Raising Monarch Butterflies (feeling joy while doing good in the world)

People, objects, and events come into one's life with a purpose, and unless we look closely, we don't notice repeating experiences or appreciate the importance of event similarities and connections. As I look back through my life, I've been made aware of how often monarch butterflies have made their appearance through the years, and appreciate their great significance in my life today. Initially, as a kid, I can often remember running through the meadows, trying to catch the beautiful monarch butterfly as it danced in the sunshine. Then, in my early years of marriage, during a Sunday drive through our neighbourhood, I spotted a monarch butterfly, got excited, and called out to my husband to look, which resulted in a fender bender collision. Not the best monarch experience but none the less a lasting monarch memory. My next monarch experience was at a backyard barbeque, when a monarch butterfly was circling the garden. I stretched out my pointed finger, and sweetly called for it to have a rest. The butterfly landed on my finger and then lingered for longer than I expected, while everyone stood and watched in awe—an incredible monarch moment.

Very soon after I met Carol, I learned that she had a hobby of raising monarch butterflies, and she brought her cage of monarchs to my townhouse. It was a perfect time to try out my new digital camera, and take pictures of the newly emerged monarch as it rested on the flowers on my front porch. Little did I know then that I would become so interested in monarch butterflies that I would devote a major part of my life, alongside Carol, learning about, raising, and protecting monarchs.

Throughout our relationship, over the last 15 years, Carol has taken the leading role, and raised, read about, researched, photographed, and documented many aspects on how to raise monarch butterflies. Much of our time is spent in nature, hiking through the ravines, while following the riverbed, and walking in parklands and along railroad tracks, looking for milkweed, in hopes of finding a monarch egg or caterpillar to take home. We would raise, tag, and release them, so we could watch them take off for their 3000 km flight to Mexico. From June to September, each year, our dining room table (Carol calls it our living laboratory) is covered with plastic containers and special cages for our monarchs. We belong to the Toronto Entomology Association, and take pride in being citizen scientists. Carol's long time fascination in raising monarch butterflies, together with the new freedom of taking thousands and thousands of pictures, blossomed into a dedicated passion. In 2015, she wrote the book, *How to Raise Monarch Butterflies, A Step-by-Step Guide for Kids,* https://www.amazon.com /Raise-Monarch-Butterflies-Step-Step/dp/1770850023, which has sold over 30,000 copies, and is referred to as the gold standard in schools when teaching kids how to raise monarch butterflies.

Carol's professional name, best known on her Facebook page, is The Monarch Crusader, where she has thousands of Facebook friends from around North America, who all have the same goal. These online connections have become friends and supporters of the monarch and insect world, all helping to improve the global environment. Carol continues to lead the way in the raising, reporting, teaching, and preservation of monarch butterflies. It's with her on-going visions, actions, and speaking engagements that she has become a knowledgeable and respected advocate in the insect world.

I love the term Carol coined in her book: Discover it, Love it, Protect it.

I feel joy and a sense of purpose when participating alongside Carol when preserving monarch butterflies and the environment. I know that this, too, creates my joy to strengthen my health.

Anything and Everything Is Possible: It's Yours to Create
(Think it, Ask for it, Believe it, See it, Do it, Have it)

You will notice that those who speak most of prosperity, have it. Those who speak most of health, have it. Those who speak most of sickness, have it. Those who speak most of poverty, have it. It is Law. It can be no other way... The way you feel is your point of attraction, and so, the Law of Attraction is most understood when you see yourself as a magnet getting more and more of the way you feel. When you feel lonely, you attract more loneliness. When you feel poor, you attract more poverty. When you feel sick, you attract more sickness. When you feel unhappy, you attract more unhappiness. When you feel healthy and vital and alive and prosperous—you attract more of all of those things.
Abraham Excerpted from "The Law of Attraction, The Basics of the Teachings of Abraham" #649

My neighbour's daughter, Angel, is an incredible inspiration to me, and she has just turned 21 years old. She was born with Down's syndrome, and throughout her life, she's had devastating health challenges. She's had many life threatening surgeries, and has just completed her chemotherapy, coming out on the other side of leukaemia. During those 21 years, she's been deeply loved and cared for by her family and my 3 daughters. Also, in those years, she's competed in down hill skiing in the Special Olympics, and won 2 medals. She performs in synchronized swimming, and is excellent in art, and great at cliff jumping, water skiing, and horseback riding. She's now in the culinary program at Humber College, and has a part time job in the kitchen of a well-known Toronto restaurant. But to my amazement, most recently, she's written and published a cookbook, *Angel's Touch* (her own recipes), with all proceeds going to The Sick Children's Hospital, in Toronto—which brings me to why I've included Angel here. I asked Angel to sign her cookbook during her recent book launch. She asked me what I'd like her to write in it, and I replied, "Write,

Anything is Possible." She cocked her head, looked at me, winked, and said, enthusiastically, "I'm going to write, *Everything is Possible.*" I turned to her, gave her a hug, and said "You are so right, Angel; and you have proven it. Everything is possible!" Angel is always about joy, and loves her life.

For many years, my friends, family, patients, and even strangers, have said to me, "You should write a book, Audrey," after hearing small snippets of my health challenges, and now, my coming out story. The same people said that they wanted to share my story with the LGBTQ people, and their families. They also said that they wanted to understand how they could be more positive, and work on being healthier. Now that I'm on the last page, having relived my journey on paper, I'm confident to repeat that we can choose to create the joy in our lives, and when we feel authentic joy, health does follow. I, too, understand that everything is possible, because there are so many things in my life that I would have thought might not be possible, and they were possible. I want to leave you with my basic beliefs, in the hope that they work for you as well as they do for me.

- I understand I am what I think; I can create how I feel by what I do.
- I can manifest and choose to live the authentic life I love.
- My emotions are my vibrational indicators toward my health.
- I know that exercise is the key component to better health.
- Health challenges are the signals urging me to think differently and make changes.
- When I think happy thoughts, and I think and live a healthy lifestyle, I create my joyful and healthy life.

Lastly,

- Be yourself.
- Take care of yourself and others.
- Love yourself and others.

- Dream Big.
- Be the star of your dreams.

In the end, everything will be OK;
if it is not OK, then it is not the end.
(1964) Paulo Coelho

I'm OK, Living Happily Ever After
(And Even This Is Not)

The End

About the Author

Audrey Kouyoumdjian spent 22 years, while secretly going from Straight to Gay, demonstrating her passion for positivity. As an author, physiotherapist, physiotherapy lecturer and business entrepreneur, Audrey enhances the lives of her family, friends, patients, colleagues, and all the people around her who wish to find and embrace joy and health.

Audrey earned her B.Sc. PT degree from the University of Toronto. She owned and operated a multidisciplinary rehabilitation practice, and now works as an in-home physiotherapist, treating patients with her hands, heart, and spirit. She lives in Toronto, Canada, with her partner of 15 years, Carol Pasternak. She enjoys frequent visits from her 3 adult children, and 3 adult stepchildren, who all live in Toronto. When she is not busy with her family, she is curling, connecting with her friends, and traveling.

To see more: google Audrey Kouyoumdjian and go to: www.straighttogaybook.com